MODERN

CONVENIENCES

THAT WOULD'VE

REWRITTEN

HISTORY

RIYA AARINI

ISBN: 978-1-956496-34-5 (paperback)
ISBN: 978-1-956496-35-2 (eBook)
Library of Congress Control Number: 2023908566
First published in Austin, Texas, USA

Visit www.riyapresents.com

CONTENTS

Part III: The Flourishing Years

INTRODUCTION

We live in the most physically comfortable era humankind has ever known. Almost every human need can be satisfied by opening the freezer, popping a pill, or indulging in the inexhaustible fun offered by the ever-widening range of inventive smartphone apps. No one in history ever imagined the extent of comfort, ease, and immediacy that all our modern conveniences deliver.

Though society prospers as a direct result of a slew of modern conveniences, people could benefit from more appreciation of these enhancements. Even the best of modern conveniences is taken for granted. Beleaguered by irritations and unhappiness, folks complain, simply because they lack the insight into how our ancestors struggled daily without access to everything we now have. Not many of us would willingly undergo major surgery without modern anesthesia, but it wasn't unheard of for ancient people to do just that. Few of us fully appreciate the cleansing powers of baking soda or the impressive durability of performance socks or even the lifesaving capabilities of electric shavers. These are present-day conveniences that historical figures never had the chance to experience.

But by becoming aware of how early humankind lived with minimal comfort—and even distress—it inspires a wholehearted sense of gratitude for the relief modern conveniences bring. In fact, those whose gratitude has run low will find it quickly replenished after perusing the historical anecdotes throughout this book. The diverse range of topics is intended to illustrate just how comparatively at ease today's societies are.

Early humans lacked a practical understanding of what would realistically alleviate their discomforts, because they didn't realize their uneasiness could've been significantly improved. None of America's daring Pony Express riders conceived of a more lightning-fast way to send letters to the opposite coast, because email didn't exist in the nineteenth century. In their eyes, the rough-and-tough riders were the speediest mail deliverers the country had ever witnessed. Even entertainment is more accessible in contemporary times. Mozart would've laughed his periwig off with the constant barrage of far-flung jokes from joke-of-the-day apps, but had to rely on a select choice of toilet humor from his immediate social circle. Even history's musical geniuses—and all its geniuses—grappled with limitations.

Early humans didn't know what they were missing. They never imagined how modern conveniences, from dental implants to social media and healthcare robots, would've enhanced their daily toil. The same can be assumed for society today—we'll never know what we're missing, until future conveniences let us in on their well-held secrets.

With this book in hand, sink into the plush cushions of a smart sofa—or a comparable piece of contemporary furniture—gain an understanding about the everyday life struggles of unwitting historical figures, and experience a profound sense of gratitude for the modern conveniences that have remarkably improved the lives of ordinary people everywhere.

PART I: THE PRIMITIVE YEARS

1

ALEXANDER THE GREAT AND ANTIBIOTICS

One of the most renowned conquerors of all time, Alexander the Great built his empire over twelve years of continuous battles ranging from the familiar home front in Greece to the exotic mountain landscapes of Asia. Merely in his early twenties in 336 B.C.E., the young Alexander controlled a loyal army that followed him into ruthless wars raged and won in the Mediterranean, the Persian Empire (including western Asia and Egypt), Afghanistan and the Khyber Pass in northern India. The youthful Macedonian king emerged victorious over kingdoms that, when combined, spanned two million square miles. Alexander the Great's voracious appetite for conquering nations was partly instilled by his father, Philip of Macedon, a remarkable ruler in his own right. It didn't hurt that the dashing young warrior picked up a lesson or two in the philosophy of warfare from his childhood tutor, Aristotle.

With his uninterrupted twelve-year winning streak, Alexander the Great couldn't be defeated—or so his soldiers and contemporaries thought. It wasn't until a particularly drunken night, at a lavish party fit for a king, that Alexander met his fate. Surrounded by sweet red wine and water, he drank as passionately as he fought, eventually falling into a slumber so deep that he would ultimately never wake up [1].

Alexander the Great had contracted typhoid, perhaps by consuming contaminated water or eating contaminated delicacies [1]. In his uncharacteristic weakness, Alexander the Great grew deathly feverish, suffered headaches, bore physical aches and pains, and could barely be roused. Lethargy struck, and the undefeatable ruler could see in his last hours his life slowly slipping from his firm grasp. On giving his soldiers a final greeting with only a flutter of his eyes, he died on June 13, 323 B.C.E.

The godlike king did not win his last battle: his fight with typhoid fever. Had Alexander the Great had access to a modern convenience—antibiotics—he would've surely survived. A tiny one-inch, dual-colored pill would have improved the king's symptoms within two days, completely curing him of his fever within a week. After a week's dose, and some rest in his tent, Alexander the Great would've regained his indomitable strength, recovering enough to resume his rapacious warfare over the endless miles of populated hills and valleys farther east. With the help of antibiotics, the king would've undoubtedly possessed the vigorous health to push onward and upward, fighting and winning wars throughout the rest of India, before moving eastward to conquer Mongolia and China. With a course of antibiotics, Alexander the Great would've not only dominated a larger sea of wealthy kingdoms around the world, but he'd have lived to rule over them all. Instead, the realms he conquered crumbled to pieces soon after his death.

Had antibiotics been available to Alexander the Great in 323 B.C.E., Hellenistic culture would have spread farther and wider than it did while he was alive, thereby influencing the world in ways that would be apparent even today. The spread of Greek language and the Greek style of education for mind and body would have given sophisticated citizens of the world a satisfying alternate cultural experience [2]. Literature, architecture, philosophical and political discourses, and theater would've been largely and fortuitously shaped by Hellenism, promoting an admirably cosmopolitan way of life [2].

But the era of antibiotics started over 2,000 years after Alexander the Great breathed his final breath. Antibiotics became available only as recently as 1928, and have since served as the tiny but powerful savior of numerous eminent and common people alike. It's worthwhile to speculate. What a harmoniously diverse world it would've been had the little pill been invented two thousand years earlier and Alexander the Great achieved his unifying vision for the world, paving the road for Hellenistic culture to permeate all parts of the globe like water through a dry sponge. It goes without saying: we ought to be thankful for the modern conveniences we enjoy today.

2

PREHISTORIC NATUFIAN BAKERS AND
BREAD MACHINES

Fourteen thousand years ago, in the grassy uplands of present-day Jordan, an ecstatic tribe of hunter-gatherers known as
Natufians lit a fire in the center of a circle built with large rocks.
They smacked together a flat patty comprised of wild wheat and
water onto a heated slab of stone, and watched the mouth-water-
ing concoction bake to heavenly perfection [1].

It was the Middle Stone Age period, just after the Old Stone Age
and before the New Stone Age. Rather than spend all their time
risking their lives chasing and hunting massive wild animals with
handmade spears, these early humans decided to sit down and take
a much-needed break. The Natufian men and women reclined on
stones, just outside the mouths of their caves. Upon visually scan-
ning their immediate surroundings, they noticed an abundance of
plants around them. Growing in the front yards of their caves were
einkorn, a type of wild wheat, and club-rush tubers [1].

A maverick in food production, one of these prehistoric men
decided to harvest the wild wheat and bring a few clusters back
to the cave. His female companions shook the clusters to dislodge
small stones or stubborn insects latched onto the stalks. The Natufian women shook the wheat berries until the outer layers dropped

off. After removing the husks, the females asked the men to join them in grinding the wheat. Both parties ground the wheat against stone, producing flour. The women once again took charge, adding water to the flour, then producing an elastic dough. Using hands strengthened by years of harvesting berries, nuts, and seeds, the women kneaded the pliable dough.

As the male members of the hunter-gatherer tribe relaxed outside, leisurely chewing on stalks of wheat, the females directed them to build a fire—if they wanted bread. Grunting, the tough Natufian men assembled heavy rocks into circle, forming a pit. The experienced fire-makers strategically packed the rocks as tightly as possible, since a close-fitting structure retained the most heat. Banging flint stones together, the males built a fire blazing at 500 degrees Fahrenheit. As the fire raged, they eyed the flames, and slapped each other prehistoric high-fives.

Rolling their eyes at the men's boyish behavior, the Natufian women casually walked out of the cave holding the flattened dough. The men snatched the dough and threw it on the heated stone protruding from the fire pit. Within twenty minutes, the bread had baked. The males rushed over to grab the bread from the heated stone—until with looks of scorn, the Natufian females snatched it away. In order to preserve their reputation as sophisticated bakers, the women had to ensure the bread was fully cooked before it was eaten. They tore open the flat bread, looking it over for signs of even baking; the crust mustn't have been burned, and the inside mustn't have been doughy. After a thorough examination, the females gave everyone a thumb's up—and the bread was immediately enjoyed by the entire tribe.

Our prehistoric hunter-gatherer ancestors savored the taste and texture of bread. Since the baking process was highly labor-intensive, bread was reserved as a special treat [1]. Occasionally, they'd throw in wild mustard seeds, other spices, or a few oats for pizzazz. Such tasty condiments, though, were reserved for when the Natufians entertained special guests, such as wandering Neanderthals or Denisovans looking for food, shelter, and friendly faces in the vicinity [1, 2].

And because the Natufians relished bread, they wanted more of it [1]. One forward-thinking member of the tribe had the bright idea of settling down permanently and growing more wild wheat. "Why not? Then we eat bread every day!" Upon announcing his grand scheme, the entire tribe leaped up and down in pure joy. The men and women worked the fields to grow wild wheat, beginning the age of agriculture.

Now, bread-making would have been a much easier endeavor if only the Natufians had access to one modern convenience—the bread machine, invented by African American entrepreneur Joseph Lee in the agriculturally advanced era of the late 1800s [3]. His cleverly built contraption would have made bread-making far less of a chore, performing tasks the Natufians tired of. Bread had to be kneaded thoroughly. Aging women hunter-gatherers likely suffered from arthritic fingers, and the men's hands could've been injured during hunts. In either case, the bread machine would have saved the day.

And a modern bread machine makes not only enough bread to feed an entire tribe of hungry hunter-gatherers, it also prepares an exquisite assortment of other fine foods. Why stop at bread, when the Natufians could have prepared cakes, banana bread, and jam—all within the three-quart capacity of the bread machine? The tribe didn't have to stop hunting either, because the bread machine would have cooked their meat too. A pound of woolly mammoth sausage and bison meatballs, dressed in locally harvested spices and sauce, would have satisfied the huge appetites of prehistoric men and women.

Entire meals could have been prepared in a single bread machine, from bread rolls to stuffing and potatoes, making entertaining foreign tribes a cinch! Running a bread machine in the blistering heat of summer wouldn't have uncomfortably overheated their caves. Being self-enclosed, the machine would keep itself cool, as well as the immediate environment. Within the versatile bread machine, all those summer berries that Natufian women picked could have been baked into a tasty blueberry cobbler.

Why settle for boring bread when early tribes could've dressed up their hot-cross buns with a savory, tantalizing artichoke dip? All that was necessary was to stuff the bread machine with artichoke hearts, a little homemade mayo and cheese, then press start. They'd go off to gather strawberries, then return an hour later to a creamy, flavorful dip. This modern convenience would've allowed early humans living in the Middle Stone Age to enjoy bread every day, like many of us do today. Being a major time-saver, the bread machine would've given our prehistoric ancestors plenty of free time to lounge around and perhaps invent even more new and original essentials, the likes of which we'd still see and enjoy. Our ancient human ancestors were the first ones to invent bread, after all. And who in contemporary society doesn't relish a helping of this rustic food with origins in prehistoric times?

3

HIPPOCRATES AND ELECTRONIC MEDICAL RECORDS

The practice of medicine wasn't always based on close patient observation, pharmacology, and surgical intervention. Rather, in ancient times, treating an ill person involved relying on superstitious beliefs, invoking the supernatural, and appealing for the mercy of the gods [1]. This was especially so in Greece before 460 B.C.E., when Hippocrates catapulted into the world and altered the course of medicine.

Greece's wisest physician, Hippocrates was born into a family of doctors—which instantly qualified him to practice medicine [1]. In ancient Greece, professional training wasn't necessary; rather, anyone with family ties to medicine could self-proclaim themselves to be a skilled physician [1]. Greek priests also practiced a sort of medicine, mixing practical knowledge with the mysteries of magic and superstition.

Hippocrates, however, broke from this long-standing tradition of giving anyone with a doctor in the family the privilege of caring for the sick. Instead, he opened a school of medicine, the School of Kos, training tuition-paying students and mandating that they take the famous Hippocratic Oath [1].

Hippocrates' many medical treatises were housed in the Great Library of Alexandria, only to be lost in later years to a fire that destroyed the building and its collections [1]. His approaches to medicine, which he noted in his books, differed starkly from his medical contemporaries and forerunners.

Personal attributes and life experience determined the nature of medical treatments Hippocrates prescribed. Naturally, each patient differed from his neighbor in this regard. A person's gender, age, habits, way of life, and place of residence guided the physician's choice of remedy [1]. Lifestyle was a crucial component for treating sickness. Hippocrates examined the person as a whole, rather than the disease itself. Cures and treatments were discovered by altering food, exercise habits, or general lifestyle. Hippocrates believed that sun therapies, sleep quality, massages, and baths could alleviate symptoms of illness—a theory that still holds true, since a healthy lifestyle is known to prevent diseases and support treatments [1].

But the most vital contribution to medicine was Hippocrates' immaculate record-keeping of patients' symptoms, illnesses, and disease progressions [1]. Prior to Hippocrates, physicians kept only oral records of the factors surrounding sickness [1]. For example, a doctor before the time of Hippocrates orally noted the symptoms of a patient's fever: chills, body aches, fatigue, and sweating. All would've been reasonably well and good until later, when the doctor might mistakenly recall the patient's temperature as being 101 degrees Fahrenheit rather than a deadly 108 degrees Fahrenheit. The highly feverish patient would've died miserably without immediate medical attention—a direct and ill-fated result of the wildly inaccurate practice of orally recollecting health symptoms.

Hippocrates overcame this glaring flaw in medicine by ensuring that he and his disciples made detailed written records of the people for whom they cared. Together, they discussed and evaluated the recorded symptoms, then arrived at a possible diagnosis and suitable treatment [1]. By relying on these clinical observations—a first for physicians everywhere—Hippocrates automatically elevated medicine to new and glorious heights [1]. His advancements earned him recognition as the father of medicine.

Now, had Hippocrates only had access to a modern convenience—the electronic medical record—his work as physician would have been significantly upgraded. While Hippocrates transformed medicine by keeping written patient records, the electronic version would have streamlined his practice a hundred-fold. Electronic medical records would've provided a level of accuracy not found in ineligible notes scribbled on papyrus. Records written on papyrus could have been easily lost due to the degradation of the material from heat, humidity, and ravenous mice. But resistant electronic medical records would have allowed ancient Greek physicians access to patient information and facilitated ongoing care, no matter the weather conditions or the number of pests.

Furthermore, Hippocrates and his disciples would've had the important opportunity to carefully analyze patient data upon reviewing symptoms presented accurately in the electronic medical records. The plague, which was a prevalent outcome of infectious disease in ancient Greece, likely wouldn't have been misdiagnosed by doctors who reviewed detailed electronic medical records [2]. Deadly plague symptoms, like fever, chills, weakness, and abdominal pain, wouldn't have been mistaken for the treatable flu [2].

Upon prescribing drugs (which in ancient times involved pulverizing the roots of herbs, such as mandrake, opium poppy, or Frankincense-tree, then extracting their oils or juices) the electronic medical records would have prevented gross medication errors [3]. Even inhaled drugs, like those from burnt plants, would have delivered the desired results when the dosage was correctly documented in the electronic medical records. Without such a modern convenience, medication errors would've been ubiquitous [5]. And an excessive number of medication errors would have not only led to physical and psychological suffering, but created an unfortunate rift between patient and physician, eroding trust in the professional relationship. The esteemed father of medicine wanted nothing of the sort.

Most importantly, the electronic medical records would have meticulously preserved the data that Hippocrates effortfully and thoughtfully gleaned from each of his disease-stricken patients. He and his disciples would have been able to engage in clinical reasoning, while encountering fewer major obstacles on the road to prescribing effective treatment. Records written hastily on papyrus simply wouldn't have made the grade. Unquestionably, Hippocrates would have placed full faith in the electronic medical records system, had it been available to physicians in the fourth century B.C.E.

4

NEANDERTHALS AND GPS

Living in complex social groups and coordinating large-scale hunts, Neanderthals regularly satisfied their need for animal protein. Lumbering across the fields were enormous woolly mammoths with giant white tusks, as well as woolly rhinoceroses [1]. The diet of Neanderthals also included the meat of wild horses, belligerent bulls that have now gone extinct, and even elephants [1].

Granted, thrusting a handmade wooden spear into these ginormous beasts would have required a series of highly strategic steps and the cooperation of multiple athletic Neanderthals. When opportunistic lions or hyenas competed with them for a sizeable portion of the meat and fat, the Neanderthals increased their risk for injury or death by a hundred-fold [1].

Ambush was likely the method our ancient hominid relatives utilized to surround their prey and bring them crashing to the ground. Hiding in the camouflaging brush for hours, waiting for an unsuspecting herd to amble on by, clearly proved to be successful. While it was risky to engage in close-range hunting, the rewards of using this technique were high: several days of sizzling prime steaks for the whole group, at every meal [1]. After all, a woolly mammoth weighing six massive tons produced a bountiful harvest of red meat that could be seared over a hot rock or roasted over a fire pit and heartily consumed.

But following a herd from a safe distance would've been challenging, since it would have taken the Neanderthals a long way from their preferred settlement. In its lifetime, a herd of woolly mammoths could travel 50,000 miles—and nonstop travel was probably not on the top of the Neanderthals' list of things to do. Neanderthals, like a significant number of us today, were homebodies and preferred to relax in the comfort of their cozy caves, pick berries from bushes, pluck nuts from pecan trees, and drink fresh water from nearby streams. It was an idyllic life—minus the excitement of the aggressive, life-threatening hunts.

Meat, however, was a mainstay in the Neanderthals' diets. Fresh animal meat provided a range of nutrients, from protein and iron to zinc and vitamin B12. Meat and its byproducts of fur and fat were essential to their way of life. But rather than wait for days for a herd of wild horses or elephants to randomly appear, Neanderthals would've fared better with a modern convenience, something like today's global positioning system, otherwise known as GPS.

The GPS is a well-known tracking system that reveals the specific location of a tracked object or, in this case, a herd of wild animals. The device operates using satellite technology. At least three satellites above earth are necessary to deliver the most precise location anywhere on land or sea. This data is transmitted to a phone or PC, and a precise location is instantly revealed. Nothing could've been more practical for the resourceful Neanderthals than to have had the opportunity to rely on GPS to hunt woolly mammoths and fallow deer.

A bold Neanderthal would simply have had to sneak up behind a woolly mammoth, attach the tracking device to its hind leg, then bolt to safety without being kicked in the face or flattened to a pancake. In a matter of minutes, the exact locations of the herd would've been available at all times on the Neanderthals' laptops. Inside their secluded, darkened cave, they'd have eagerly gathered around the amply lit touchscreen, analyzed the movements of the herd, assigned specific roles of attack to each of their fellow hominids based on the configuration of the individual animals within the herd—and, in short, make their job of hunting a piece of raspberry lemon cake.

No more waiting in earnest for a sizeable animal worth its meat to amble on by and be swiftly speared. Neanderthals using GPS would've been similar to today's youth relying on GPS to find the location of the latest, hottest dining establishment. Indeed, the availability of GPS 130,000 years ago would have been akin to Neanderthals having mobile fast-food restaurants at their fingertips twenty-four hours a day. The wild herds they hunted wouldn't have become displaced by the worsening effects of the then-present climate change, allowing the Neanderthal species with GPS the means to continue tracking and hunting successfully, and perhaps surviving to live side by side among us today.

Unmistakably, our hominid cousins would've had no trouble using GPS to navigate their thousands of miles of untamed hills and valleys to reach vital meat sources. After all, Neanderthals were highly intelligent—smart enough to have thrived as a species 200,000 years longer than modern-day humans.

5

NEFERTITI'S EGYPT AND STICK DEODORANT

Nefertiti reigned over Egypt with husband Pharaoh Akhenaten from 1353 to 1336 B.C.E. The king and queen strategically shifted their capitol to the greener pastures of Amarna, where Akhenaten ruled for seventeen eventful years [1]. Dodging cultural turmoil, the couple spent their lives smitten in each other's affectionate company. Nefertiti took center stage in a series of wall paintings, enjoying life with Akhenaten and undertaking activities reserved only for privileged rulers [1]. Their union produced six healthy daughters, two of whom later became Egyptian queens [2]. Since Nefertiti gave birth to no sons, Akhenaten took other wives. A male heir, King Tut—Nefertiti's stepson—was born.

The New Kingdom flourished, and its grand wealth financed the construction of towering pyramids the heights of which would be nearly impossible to reach even today. Laborers built opulent tombs gilded in gold, with walls of hieroglyphics telling wondrous stories about the blessed life and afterlife.

While the king and queen were vital to Egypt, the lifeblood of the nation was its citizenry. In daily life, the wealthy ancient Egyptian elites threw ceremonious banquets that catered to hundreds of merrymaking guests. Social gatherings and parties took place to celebrate this world and beyond. Of course, with ancient Egypt being a highly civilized society, it was essential to follow social etiquette.

Summer temperatures in ancient Egypt soared to 95 degrees Fahrenheit [3]. The sticky, hot weather caused heavy perspiration not only among the laboring classes growing crops and herding animals, but the social elites celebrating their wealth. The resourceful Egyptians wouldn't stand for unpleasant body odor and devised a curious solution: the head cone.

Ancient Egyptians handmade three-inch tall head cones out of beeswax, which lower classes could afford. Upper-class citizens resorted instead to unguent. Both materials superbly perfumed their wearers. How so? Simply, the wax was fashioned into a cone and secured on top of the head. In the blazing heat of Egypt, the wax melted, cleansing and perfuming the hair and body. Problem solved: no more noxious body odor to dissuade guests from gathering in close quarters.

Eons passed before archaeologists proved that wax head cones were more than simply imagined, as they'd originally been seen only in paintings on tomb walls [4]. Hieroglyphics showed men and women adorned in head cones; emanating curved lines suggested the cones released an aromatic scent [5]. Recent excavations of a grave of a lower-class Egyptian woman between 1337 and 1332 B.C.E. revealed the truth: head cones were indeed worn in ancient Egypt [4]. Since the woman was buried with her head cone, archaeologists concluded that if she smelled good enough, she was fit to dwell with the gods in the afterlife. No stinky individuals were admitted to the eternal hereafter.

Now, had a modern convenience—stick deodorant—been available to Nefertiti's subjects, the head cone would've been unnecessary. A wax head cone, no matter how carefully strapped to the head, was cumbersome. It could slip, topple to the ground, and crumble, rendering it useless. How many hours on a summer day or night could a three-inch cone of wax realistically last, anyway? Furthermore, sweet-smelling ancient Egyptians on their death beds could rest assured that the gods would welcome them into the afterlife without a blink of an eye or a repulsed twist of the nose. Stick deodorant would've suited the social etiquette needs and eternal afterlife protocol of ancient Egyptians.

While various means of controlling body odor were in use since the advent of humanity, it wasn't until the late nineteenth century that deodorant became widely available. Similar to ancient Egyptian head cones, deodorant was manufactured out of wax, albeit with the addition of oils and silicones. In 1888, in the United States, the first paste used to control the smell of perspiration consisted of a waxy cream [6]. Less than two decades later, stick deodorant was available on store shelves, and encouraged for use by all well-mannered individuals. Stick deodorant kept hardworking men and women smelling fresh for hours.

The one-to-two million subjects over whom Nefertiti ruled in Amarna would've enjoyed nothing better than to be liberated from self-consciousness by wearing stick deodorant when attending overcrowded religious ceremonies and spontaneous social gatherings. The queen herself wouldn't have declined the golden opportunity to smell shower-fresh wherever her royal duties happened to lead her. This modern convenience would've allowed ancient Egyptians to be in good company without complaint during the hottest of summer months. But it took nearly 3,000 years since the dawn of wax head cones for stick deodorant to be invented—and we in contemporary society are relieved it finally was.

6

STONEHENGE BUILDERS AND CONSTRUCTION ROBOTS

Since its Neolithic construction completion 5,000 years ago, the circle of monolithic stones in southern England's Salisbury Plain has stood as an enigma. Erected to reach the heavens, Stonehenge was the towering skyscraper of its time, amazing visitors from miles away. While its significance remains only partially understood, how it was built still mystifies people all over the civilized world.

Stonehenge wasn't built in a jiffy, not in a heartbeat, and definitely not in a year. The colossal stones were erected over a painfully prolonged period of 1500 years [1]. That's sixty generations of the Neolithic builders' descendants who remained unwaveringly committed to hoisting the enormous non-indigenous bluestones and sarsen sandstone slabs to gradually form the structure. The marvel of Stonehenge was not how it was built, but the dedication of its builders for over a millennium.

Transporting the sarsen sandstone from the quarries to the sacred site was a monumental task, considering the largest weighed forty tons and stood twenty-four feet high [2]. The number of mythical stories that offer possible explanations for how Stonehenge was built were far worthier of the imagination than the practical solutions builders might have employed.

King Arthur's Merlin, for instance, was believed to have positioned the gigantic rocks of Stonehenge perfectly with a wave of his wand and the words of his magic spell [1]. The wizard's sorcery brought the Giants' Ring, a stone circle of African bluestones, across the sea to Salisbury Plain [1]. The fallen British nobles who were slaughtered by the Saxons rested in a fitting burial place for eternity [1]. King Arthur felt so awed by the grandeur of Stonehenge that he buried his beloved father, Uther, there too [1].

Yet science demonstrates Stonehenge was built many millennia before the legend of King Arthur entered the minds of early Britons [1]. Science also offers other construction theories. During an Ice Age, glaciers could have carried the massive slabs 200 miles to an area near Salisbury Plain, coincidentally depositing the right number to complete the perfect circle [1]. Or perhaps Neolithic builders stumbled upon glacial erratics on the plain and finished Stonehenge. But crushing this geological theory is the fact that ice sheets may have never actually reached Salisbury Plain [1].

Some say extraterrestrial beings could have made a special visit a few thousand years ago to help the struggling Britons build their masterpiece [1]. The aliens would have benefitted, too, since the stone circle would have doubled as a landing pad for their spacecraft [1]. But no one in contemporary times has ever proved the existence of helpful green Martians boasting superior engineering knowledge, nor is there evidence of any advanced airship landing in the grassy plains of south England.

Then there are the more practical explanations of how the miraculous Stonehenge was erected. Small, rotating rocks could've been used to transport the mega-ton slabs of stone—which would have taken an hour to move a mere 300 feet [1]. While Stone Age technology had its merits, other techniques held water as well. Stone balls combined with wooden planks could have been used to slide the stone blocks to their final destination within two weeks [1]. Finally, wicker cage contraptions could've been fashioned out of natural materials available at the time and served to roll the stones over the long distances [1].

Exactly how Neolithic Britons constructed Stonehenge remains an unsolvable mystery. What's most impressive is that the original builders successfully convinced generations of descendants to continue the project, showing admirable skills in persuasion. Only a few cremated remains, approximately fifty-eight, have been unearthed at Stonehenge [3]. This means the significance of the burial site surpassed the demanding level of physical exertion required to build it.

Stonehenge was intended to be a contemplative place, one to which the descendants of long-gone Neolithic people could retire to recognize and honor the lives of their departed ancestors. And memorializing those who had gone before us had been a custom woven into the fabric of human society since the time of the Neanderthals, who also ceremoniously buried their dead. So this argument could have been used to persuade builders to sweat and toil for over a thousand years.

Now, erecting Stonehenge could have been completed in a far quicker time span, if only the Neolithic builders and their architects had access to the modern convenience of construction robots. Rather than wait more than a millennium to see the final outcome of their perseverance and hard work, the prehistoric Britons could've enjoyed the fruits of their labor within a matter of weeks.

Envisioning the dream was the first step in any human endeavor. A construction robot would've been used to draw up a digital architectural plan. The robot's all-terrain tracks would've crawled over hills of grass to dutifully follow the Neolithic builders to their carefully chosen destination of Salisbury Plain. Robotic excavation systems would've effortlessly excavated the holes for the insertion of the timber posts. The robot would've allowed for precision leveling, within one millimeter, to ensure that the slabs didn't tilt in an undignified manner. If Briton's ancient builders wanted sections of stone finished with paint, the robots would've capably spray-painted these areas without complaint. The arms of the construction robots would've sanded the rough slabs of stone to smooth perfection—and the day's work would've been completed with a battery charge of eight hours.

But the construction industry was digitally transformed only in the twenty-first century—5,000 years after the Neolithic Britons erected the first mega-slab in their multi-stone ceremonial structure. The prehistoric builders would've remained safer, too, with the construction robots performing all the challenging labor, from picking up the five-ton boulders to positioning them in place per the detailed specifications in the digital architectural design. Safety measures would've also protected the builders from being flattened to a patty, had a precariously standing slab of stone unexpectedly crashed to the ground. Like today, it'd have taken only a handful of Neolithic builders to oversee the entire building of the massive monument. Instead of taking 1500 years to raise Stonehenge, construction robots would've accelerated it to a mere two weeks.

7

HAMMURABI AND SMART TOOTHBRUSHES

Ancient Babylon, strategically positioned between the Euphrates and Tigris Rivers in present-day Iraq, was once the largest, most splendorous city in the world, boasting a population of over 100,000 [1]. Long before then, Hammurabi, the king of the first dynasty of Babylon, ruled over 25,000 Babylonians. His reign began in 1792 B.C.E. and ended upon his death in 1750 B.C.E.

Hammurabi endorsed himself as a just and equitable ruler. Women enjoyed numerous rights and freedoms, more so than their Greek counterparts in later times. Babylonian women assumed prominent public roles, like priestess and city official [1]. Many women owned their homes and took advantage of their right to pass property to their grown children [1]. Women also represented themselves in courts of law [1]. While gender equality was notable in Hammurabi's time, the king who promoted it remained occupied with a range of royal duties: building temples, constructing city walls, digging canals, and engaging in warfare with the kingdom of Larsa downstream on the Euphrates.

The Babylonian king was also renowned for firmly laying down the law in his famed Hammurabi's Code, a collection of laws engraved on a four-ton slab of stone. Hammurabi's style of retaliatory justice revolved around the premise of "an eye for an eye, and a tooth for a tooth" [2]. If a man were to knock out the tooth of an enemy in a vengeful brawl, it was justified that the aggressor's own tooth received an equally powerful blow. Such was the execution of Hammurabi's everyday social justice.

Hammurabi clearly valued a full set of teeth—after all, the very mention of "a tooth for a tooth" was meticulously carved into stone in his eminent code of laws. The king utilized the dental tools available in the eighteenth-century B.C.E. Mesopotamia to clean and ensure the longevity of his natural teeth. Ancient Babylonians, like Hammurabi, remained on top of their dental hygiene by brushing with chew sticks [3]. Since 3500 B.C.E., these wooden twigs with frayed ends were used to scrub teeth, cleaning them of trapped food particles [3]. Hammurabi owned a set of exquisite regal chew sticks, perhaps studded with precious gems, as any health-conscious king would.

Chew sticks, the ancient form of the modern-day toothbrush, were essential to the dental health of Babylonians. Seventy-foot date palms flourished along Mesopotamia's flattened lands, yielding copious amounts of the sweet, sticky fruit. Constantly munching on dates would've led to serious tooth decay. Evidently, such was the case in ancient Babylon, as Babylonians consumed a lot of dates. And why wouldn't they pick and eat the tasty fruits hanging in tantalizing clusters fifty feet in the air? Although dates contained fluorine, which reversed early tooth decay, the sticky consistency of dates caused the fruit to adhere to teeth, accelerating the development of cavities [4]. Without an effective tooth-brushing regimen, especially after consuming the dates, significant tooth loss would've occurred, as was proven upon discoveries of skeletal remains from early Mesopotamia [5].

King Hammurabi surely felt sporadic pain from consuming numerous dates and experiencing the tooth decay that would've inevitably followed. Royal records from the time do not point to this likelihood, but why announce a misfortune that could've diminished the public's idyllic view of their flawless ruler? Anyhow, the crudely made chew sticks of Babylon were ineffective in completely removing every trace of foodstuffs stuck to the teeth of ancient Babylonians, including Hammurabi. What they needed was a dental tool that was powerful, thorough, and full of important data.

Now, this dental tool is none other than the smart toothbrush—a celebrated modern convenience. A ground-breaking invention, the smart toothbrush would've given an individual an enormous amount of feedback on personal brushing technique. Brushing frequency would've been tracked, in case an ancient Babylonian forgot whether he brushed that morning or not. Awful morning breath was never enough to remind someone to perform this essential task. Pressure would've been measured, because no one wanted to brush too vigorously and brush away gums that never grew back. A convenient timer would've been installed in the smart toothbrush to inform the Babylonian exactly how long he'd been standing there brushing his teeth. A special sensor would've also been included to let him know in which quadrant he was currently brushing, in case he was unaware. A coaching app would've also been useful for fervent Babylonian tooth-brushers who wanted to up their game.

Given all the miraculous functions of the smart toothbrush, Hammurabi—and the ancient Babylonians over whom he ruled—would've enjoyed enhanced oral hygiene. They could've eaten all the dates they desired without worrying about the commonplace cavities that plagued their society. Having a smart toothbrush whirring over their teeth would've kept their pearly whites clean and cavity-free, and given them invaluable feedback on their brushing habits.

Alas, the smart toothbrush wasn't invented until 2014, over 2,000 years after Hammurabi first ordered his famous code of laws to be engraved permanently in stone. Fortunately for the oral health of today's society, the smart toothbrush is readily available and incredibly beneficial after consuming a handful of sticky Middle Eastern dates.

8

ANCIENT EGYPTIAN WIVES AND MODERN PAPER

One thing passed down since the dawn of civilization is the marriage contract. This document laid out a clear set of rules between husband and wife about how property must be divided if either spouse died or they dissolved the union. And in ancient Egypt, divorce was common.

Also like today, ancient Egyptian men were known to thrive in bachelorhood. Hekeyeb was just such a bachelor living in Egypt in 1880 B.C.E. [1]. A hieroglyphic inscription, discovered in a tomb, showed how enamored he was with living enthusiastically as a single man. He enjoyed a childhood of ease, a youth spent in the company of numerous women, and the comfort of a fine home. Hekeyeb even painted his tomb with the exquisite delights of life in preparation for his eternal afterlife [1]. Dying as an old man, he still clung fervently to his joyful bachelorhood [1].

But for those who preferred marriage, a contract was vital to protect their economic welfare. In fact, a contract was so essential, that ancient people all over the Near East declared that a wife was not a legitimate wife if a marriage contract was not in place [1]. The contract not only confirmed the marriage but impacted the children of that union. For instance, children born to an illegitimate wife failed to secure the same rights as children born to a legitimate wife [1]. And men in ancient Egypt were known to manage multiple wives, a polygamous way of life that would astound men of sane mind today. These arrangements were recognized thanks to the marriage contract.

An Egyptian woman by the name of Tneferteu, for instance, entered into a marriage contract in 263 B.C.E. [1]. The contract rolled out eight stipulations, one of which declared Tneferteu to be the wife of Paret, the son of Efow and Taret [1]. The marriage contract listed the husband's offerings, which included one silver piece intended as Tneferteu's luxurious bridal gift [1]. Also agreed in the contract was the daily amount of wheat he'd give to his wife [1]. In the unfortunate, or perhaps fortunate, event that Paret lost romantic interest in Tneferteau and abandoned her, then, according to the marriage contract, he was responsible for gifting her five more silver pieces, totaling six with the inclusion of the initial bridal gift [1]. The ancient Egyptian marriage contract also specified that half of everything Paret owned belonged fair and square to Tneferteu— including the assets he acquired from the day of the marriage, onward [1].

Marriage contracts in ancient Egypt were drawn up by a male proposing marriage, or by a female ready to tie the knot [1]. In either case, the purpose of the contract was to protect the financially weaker spouse [1]. If a legitimate wife lost the marriage contract, she could expect financial trouble.

Ancient Egyptian marriage contracts were written on papyrus. Using papyrus to note records began in 3000 B.C.E. in Egypt [2]. Out of the fertile regions grew an abundance of papyrus marshes. The papyrus plant, considered by the Egyptians to be a symbol of rebirth, flourished in damp soil in the marshes of the Nile Delta [2]. Egyptians created papyrus sheets worthy of the written word by first harvesting the stalks of the papyrus plants. They extracted the pulp or fibers, layered strips of the inner stalk and pressed them, resulting in bound layers [2]. The ancient Egyptians hammered the sheets, dried them in the sun, then carefully smoothed them with shells [2].

Sap adhered up to twenty sheets of papyrus, which were rolled around two ornately decorated wooden sticks [2]. Papyrus scrolls, among the most famous and recognizable products out of ancient Egypt, were designed for record-keeping, correspondence, and legal contracts. Of course, the twenty sheets of papyrus required for a scroll exceeded the amount necessary to create a standard marriage contract. One papyrus sheet was enough to carry the union's eight stipulations, plus a notary signature.

Although it was a lightweight writing material, papyrus wasn't durable. Under stress, papyrus tore. The nibs of ink pens would easily puncture or scratch its uneven, brittle surface, resulting in holes [2]. And safeguarding a marriage contract written on a delicate sheet of papyrus had its own set of potential hazards. The thin sheet of papyrus could have taken flight in angry gusts of wind, stored carelessly and lost, or devoured by hungry mice. The cream color of newly pressed papyrus sheets darkened with age, making the important details of the contract illegible [3]. Unless sufficiently protected, marriage contracts written on papyrus could degrade upon long-term exposure to the sun's UV rays, making the document worthless as it disintegrated into a pile of dust [3]. A legal contract that was so fragile had to be carefully spared from natural decomposition and stored with utmost conscientiousness in order to protect the financial interests of the wife and her children.

Relying on a legal document that could flake into pieces during the course of a lengthy marriage was highly chancy. Ancient Egyptian wives, who were considered equal in status to their husbands, deserved a more reliable solution: a marriage contract written on a sturdier material, like our modern convenience, paper.

But paper was only invented 2,000 years ago—a thousand years after papyrus took off in Egypt as the preferred writing material. Chinese Imperial court official Ts'ai Lun experimented with the craft of papermaking in 105 C.E. While his paper-making process remained shrouded in mystery, it was believed he prepared a concoction of water mixed with mulberry bark, hemp, and rags [4]. He mashed it to form a pulp, pressed the mass to release the moisture, then dried the sheets in the sun. Lun's secret remained well-kept until 793 C.E., when the art of papermaking spread to the Middle East [5]. Europeans got wind of paper production methods, and paper mills popped up all over Europe by the fourteenth century [5]. It wasn't until the 1800s that wood pulp came into fashion for making paper—a better option than the cotton rags in constant short supply [5]. Since wood pulp was abundantly available, papermaking grew into a large-scale production [5].

Before the ubiquity of paper machines, paper was painstakingly manufactured one sheet at a time [5]. Dramatic improvements to the machines continued from 1807 until today, when papermaking became a highly technical, advanced industry. Nowadays, paper is accessible all over the globe. Paper marriage contracts are still drawn up with the same purpose as 2,000 years ago.

Today's well-made paper has a life expectancy of centuries [6]. Indeed, some papyrus sheets dating from around 2900 B.C.E. have been discovered in ancient tombs [3]. But the inner recesses of tombs remained highly protected from the sun's harsh UV rays and extreme heat. Marriage partners in ancient Egypt, especially the lower classes, were unlikely to have equal access to such protective areas, thereby jeopardizing the conservancy of their legal contracts.

If only ancient Egyptian marriage partners had access to the modern convenience of durable, high-quality paper, marriage contracts would've been preserved far more efficiently—thereby diminishing the financial risks to women and their children if a marriage contract scribbled on papyrus was lost or terribly degraded. Of course, a contract could've been renewed. But if two Egyptian spouses by ill chance happened to be embattled in a bitter dispute and on the brink of divorce around the time the marriage contract was lost, the timing of the renewal would have been utterly disastrous. Fortunately, amid digital advancements, paper contracts still hold weight today.

9

THE GREAT LIBRARY OF ALEXANDRIA AND EBOOKS

Julius Caesar was a man of many achievements. A celebrated statesman, he transformed the notable Roman empire from its meager status as a republic. The politically savvy general granted Roman citizenship to foreigners. Caesar rose to staggering heights politically and militarily. Indeed, he came, he saw, he conquered. Not only was he renowned for his diplomatic genius, but for his intensely passionate affair with Queen Cleopatra in 48 B.C.E., near Alexandria, Egypt.

Caesar was also known for one major blunder: the accidental burning of the Great Library of Alexandria. This library was built around 295 B.C.E. by Alexander the Great's successor, Ptolemy I Soter, as part of the Museum of Alexandria. The library was situated near the harbor off the Mediterranean Sea. The museum itself was a popular destination, made attractive by its zoo of exotic animals, among them elephants, zebras, ostriches, peacocks, and pheasants [1].

The destruction of the library was an accident of huge proportions. Siding with Cleopatra, Caesar was embroiled in a civil war, defending himself and his 3200 soldiers and their 800 horses against a hostile enemy, Ptolemy XIII [2]. He knew of no defensive maneuver other than to fight with fire. He ordered his soldiers to hurl flames at the enemies' warships and their infantry of 20,000 men strong [1]. The coastal wind fanned the flames, launching the burning embers into the harbor, over the decks, and onto the rooftops of nearby homes [1]. It wasn't too long before the Great Library of Alexandria was caught in the rapidly spreading blaze. Caesar's auxiliary soldiers unintentionally destroyed the majestic library and its enormous quantity of books.

At the time, the Great Library of Alexandria held ancient scrolls numbering in the hundreds of thousands. It is estimated that the collection contained 400,000 to 700,000 books on a range of erudite topics, such as the sciences, astronomy, medicine, law, comedy, and lyric poetry [3, 4]. Egypt's Ptolemy rulers acquired the library's books, with the bulk of the collections being written in Greek or containing Egyptian histories written in the Egyptian language. Ships that entered the harbor were searched, and worthy books were confiscated or copied on the spot [3]. The Greeks were thirsty for knowledge, and the magnificent library was the culmination of their quest for the wisdom of notable minds.

The exact number of books destroyed by the fire in the Great Library of Alexandria remains in question, changing depending on the source. Seneca, for instance, claimed that 40,000 books were lost in the fire [1]. In later centuries, both Aulus Gellius and Ammianus reported that 700,000 books were burned to cinders [1]. And even later, Orosius, exhaling heavily, uttered unconsolably that 400,000 books of magnificent intellectual brilliance were destroyed [1].

The accidental burning of the Great Library of Alexandria and a significant sum of its collections was a monumental tragedy. While the fire accelerated the destruction of the books, time would have had its way, too. The papyrus scrolls would have ultimately degraded over the years as a result of exposure to coastal Mediterranean heat and humidity. Mice and pests were also likely to have chewed through the scrolls, leaving nothing but miniscule shreds of papyrus with barely decipherable handwritten letters. Many years of scholars handling the scrolls would also have led to their inevitable ruin.

Now, had a modern convenience—eBooks—been available at the time of the Great Library of Alexandria, the legacy of impressively diverse knowledge would have been saved. In fact, intellectual men and women today would still have access to the wisdom of learned thinkers since before the last millennia. Even contemporaries of the ancient world wouldn't have worried about the inevitable deterioration of their prized collections of delicately handwritten papyrus scrolls. Instead, they'd have leisurely walked around Alexandria in 48 B.C.E. investing all their attention in an eReader held in one hand, the other adjusting their robes against Mediterranean breezes. Impromptu discussions with likeminded intellectuals would've been held in the middle of Fouad Street upon voraciously consuming scholarly eBooks on the Great Library of Alexandria's ancient app. Being fire-proof, time-proof, and destruction-proof, digital books would've outlasted every existing written material. The Great Library of Alexandria's eBooks would've imparted the learnedness of philosophers, scientists, mathematicians, astronomers, and playwrights to endless generations to come.

But eBooks were only invented in 1971, over 2,000 years after Julius Caesar inadvertently burned down the Great Library of Alexandria. What an irreparable loss to cultured society that eBooks didn't exist at the time of the biggest universal library the world had ever known. Academics today would've rejoiced in the study of the original works by the eminent dramatic poets, Sophocles, Euripides, and Aeschylus. They'd have savored the multiple versions of the same Homeric texts from places like Chios and Sinope. The surviving works, after all, represented only a tiny fraction of the library's original content. The vast knowledge of the erudite world, housed precariously in the Great Library of Alexandria, would have been preserved forever.

Fortunately, today, any new knowledge or semblance of it will be safeguarded for as long as civilization relies on technology because of one modern convenience: the irreplaceable eBook.

PART II: THE LEAN YEARS

10

KING HENRY VIII AND NUTRITION APPS

In 1509, at the lithesome age of seventeen, King Henry VIII found himself crowned king of England. His ascension to the throne was met with much fanfare, as he proved to be a breath of fresh air in comparison to his stern, dry father, Henry VII.

Henry VIII lived larger than life. Not only did he tower over six feet tall, but the charming extrovert had a zest for life and lived it to its fullest glory. Under his rule, the court threw lavish parties, entertaining the worthiest of guests with scores of music he personally composed. The King's Ballad, a folk song he is reputed to have penned during a merry afternoon of feasting and drinking, was incredibly popular, sung in court as well as in taverns across the English countryside. Henry VIII savored hearty food as much as he savored life itself and gorged on a variety of delicacies, including the game he hunted. Hunting was a favorite pastime outside of his royal duties, and he made time to chase small animals to complete exhaustion while riding majestically on his magnificent, noble steed. Joisting, too, was included in his royal calendar, and he enthusiastically participated in his favored sport into his fourth decade of life.

Outside of his hobbies and musical talents, the charismatic king was equally impressive. King Henry VIII was noted as being among the handsomest rulers in all of England, if not Europe itself. The countless royal paintings show off his muscular physique under a sea of flowing royal clothing, perfectly trimmed blond facial hair and a jubilant disposition. Despite his physical strength and athleticism, though, King Henry VIII wasn't much of a conqueror. Warfare went to the wayside as he valiantly strove to produce a male heir with any of his six wives, whom he married in succession—after creating the Church of England to support his decision to divorce his very first wife, Catherine of Aragon [1].

King Henry VIII's troubles didn't begin immediately upon ascending the throne. Gregarious and popular, he fared well for quite some time. Rather, decades passed before misery made its visit, as it does in nearly every human life, of any social status. One breezy English day, when the sun hid behind the clouds, King Henry VIII decided to participate in one of his jousting tournaments. Wearing a visor and sporting a lance, he charged toward his opponent, also on horseback. Unexpectedly, the king tumbled from his horse, lying trapped under the beast [2]. King Henry VIII sustained traumatic injuries, and changed dramatically [2].

Aside from developing an irascible temperament, one of the most visible changes was the steadily increasing size of his girth [2]. Over the next eleven years, the once charming and athletic Tudor king grew substantially in bodily size, so much so that contemporaries had never seen the likes of a man weighing 400 pounds. His love for food continued, but because of his jousting accident, he could no longer exercise as he once did [2]. As he always had, though, King Henry VIII continued to eat 5,000 calories per day—twice the recommendation for a grown man.

Now, a modern convenience—the nutrition app—could've saved King Henry VIII from such an unhealthy doom. The nutrition app would've given the obese king a chance at maintaining a healthy body weight, despite having the leg injury that limited his ability to stay physically fit. A nutrition app would have performed the necessary task of helping King Henry VIII monitor his daily food intake. Rather than sample buffets daily as he pleased, the king would've felt compelled to watch his waistline and selectively pick the healthiest foods. The app would've conveniently let the king know the calorie content of every meal, perhaps giving him the motivation to strategically decide to consume less than his usual 5,000 daily calories.

Admittedly, nutrition apps are notoriously inaccurate. But the wealthy King Henry VIII could have easily commissioned a band of tech gurus to develop an app that produced correct data—or off with their heads! After all, the king hadn't batted an eye at chopping off the heads of over 70,000 people [3]. In any case, the future of England would've been at stake.

While King Henry VIII would've benefited from his nutrition app, he might have further improved his health by additionally investing in a meat tracking app. He relished meats of all kinds, like decadent pies of roasted game, venison steaks bathed in thick gravy, tender cuts of lamb, or a braised swan that had just been squawking on the lake that morning [4]. A meat tracking app would've let the Tudor king know the amount of his daily meat consumption, even helping him go meatless on sporadic days, if such a vegan thing were possible for a sixteenth-century monarch with a massively carnivorous appetite. Inadvertently, King Henry VIII would've helped preserve the environment by making the eco-friendly choice to consume less meat—instantly making yet another contribution to his remarkable royal legacy.

11

BUBONIC PLAGUE DOCTORS AND
HEALTHCARE ROBOTS

During the seventeenth century, sailors and merchants landed at the breezy port in Naples, Italy. The sun shone radiantly in the blue sky, its heat softened by cool ocean winds. Meanwhile, aboard the ships, sailors lay dead, and the living recoiled at the strange black boils on their bodies discharging blood and pus.

It was 1656, and central and southern Italy had been struck by a catastrophic wave of the Bubonic Plague. Contemporaries described the plague boils as growing to the size of "apples" or "eggs" [1]. The onslaught of blood and pus that oozed out of these boils was a frightening sight to Neapolitans who were unable to explain the terrors that besieged them. The sickened lay helpless with high fevers and chills. Vomiting and diarrhea accompanied unbearable body aches and pains. All these symptoms preceded the inevitable—a miserable death.

No one knew at the time that the Bubonic Plague was responsible for unleashing a seismic wave of unbridled terror. The disease attacked the lymphatic system, causing the lymph nodes to swell [1]. Without prompt and effective medical treatment, almost universally unavailable in Naples, the infection spread quickly to the lungs or blood [1]. A healthy Neapolitan could be picking lemons on a Saturday afternoon, become infected by the plague by evening, and die on Sunday morning.

People dropped like fleas, the likes of which were partially responsible for spreading the Bubonic Plague in Italy. Fleas infected with the germ *Yersinia pestis* would bite a human, and the unsuspecting individual would develop frightening symptoms of the plague shortly afterward [1]. Infected rats would spread terror in the same way. Since rats were especially populous onboard ships, the plague spread rapidly between European port cities, including Naples [1].

Physicians of the day were as perplexed as the patients they attempted to treat. Prevention was impossible, and effective treatments were unheard of. In efforts to avoid sickness, healthy people avoided those devastated by illness [1]. Out of similar concerns, doctors sometimes refused patients [1]. The seventeenth century medical community in Italy was flummoxed—no one could determine with any accuracy the course of this mysterious disease. All that was certain: death knocked thrice at the door of anyone infected with the plague.

The only hope Neapolitans had was in the somewhat dubious skill of their doctors. Physicians themselves couldn't explain the erratic nature of the disease, but they could recognize its symptoms. How did the dignified, educated Neapolitan doctors handle the immense faith ordinary citizens bestowed upon them? They dressed up as toco toucans, of course.

The plague costume worn by physicians in Naples during the 1656 plague outbreak was eye-catching and worthy of the exalted profession to which they had nobly committed themselves. The doctors donned an outfit made of Moroccan goat leather, complete with a long coat, breeches, boots, a hat, and gloves [2]. A set of crystal eye pieces sewn into the face mask allowed the physicians to see their patients [2]. Also part of the face mask was a six-inch-long beak [2]. Doctors carried a long stick, likely to force the sick to stay a safe distance from them. Recognized by healthy and ill Neapolitans alike, this outfit had a specific function—to protect the doctors as they hopelessly tended to the needs of the deathly ill.

The plague outfit worn by physicians served as a physical barrier that prevented environmental contaminants from entering through the skin's pores. To this end, the long coat, boots, and gloves were well-suited. The dramatically elongated beaks were especially vital to the health of the physicians. The beaks were stuffed with an assortment of intoxicating herbs, like cinnamon, pepper, turpentine, and honey, a potent combination believed to protect the beaked physicians from inhaling contaminated air [2]. The long toucan beak was practical in design, too, ensuring poisoned air would be cleansed by the aromatic herbs by the time it reached the physicians' nostrils [3].

Impressive as the Neapolitan physicians appeared while wearing their toucan beak and robe, the people of Naples held a far less admirable view of them. Doctors of the time were considered little else than frightening money-makers profiting off the dead and dying [2]. Nevertheless, physicians had enough knowledge to identify plague symptoms, which brought at least some relief to a period when there was little left to hope for. Physicians assumed the plague was spread directly from the sick or from poisons in the air. The doctors aimed to stay as far away from disease-stricken individuals as possible, while somehow delivering a respectable level of medical care.

Now, what Naples needed then was a modern convenience—the healthcare robot. This technology would've performed tasks that a Neapolitan doctor refused to do, like touching plague-ridden patients, or those showing festering symptoms. Instead of the doctor impersonally jabbing a sick individual with a stick from four feet away, the healthcare robot would've had no fear in gently shifting the person onto his side or helping him up from his bed. Skin conditions, including the nasty egg-size boils, could've been expertly evaluated by the healthcare robot's built-in infrared light [4]. Then, the robot would've communicated the seriousness of the results to the doctor himself [4]. The sick individual's room could've been fully disinfected by an automated disinfection robot using the miraculous powers of UVC light [4].

Healthcare robots have a high success rate in giving accurate diagnoses [4]. A seventeenth-century Neapolitan who suspected he'd been infected with the plague could've turned to a healthcare robot for a diagnosis that was ninety-nine percent accurate. And the Neapolitan physician who correctly programmed his healthcare robot would've eliminated all chances of failure in the technology, while providing only minimal supervision to ensure its proper functionality.

Routine check-ups would've been a piece of triple-flavored Neapolitan cake. The healthcare robot would've easily checked vital signs, including blood pressure, blood sugar, and body temperature [4]. Fevers were a common symptom of the plague, so any temperature reading above normal would've been a clear indication of infection.

All these important healthcare services would've been delivered remotely by the attending doctor. The Neapolitan physician wouldn't have had to risk his health to provide medical care to the sick and dying. Plus, his plague costume might not have been necessary at all, since he wouldn't have seen the need to enter a sick person's home and be exposed to contaminants. Some healthcare robots would've even been able to complete certain medical tasks independently, thereby eliminating the need for the in-person care the Neapolitan physicians felt so hesitant to give.

Best of all, the healthcare robots wouldn't have been as frightening as the doctors dressed up in their plague costumes. The robots would've given passersby a friendly smile with their digital heart-shaped eyes [5]. They'd have made calming cooing sounds as they passed patients, and engaged them in conversation to help them relax.

But healthcare robots are among the most recent of modern conveniences, having had their initial rollout in the twenty-first century—over 300 years after the Naples Plague. Today, routine medical tasks are being increasingly performed by robotic technology, including services that humans would rather not do. What a breath of fresh air the healthcare robot would've been to Neapolitan doctors who didn't want to jeopardize their lives while treating the era's deadliest infectious disease.

12

PERIWIG WEARERS AND BAKING SODA

Fashion trends are driven by a range of known factors, from social and political, to economic, environmental, and physiological. But one seventeenth-century hair trend emerged from the most inconceivable of influences: syphilis. Even if it may not have been identified at the time as an influence.

Europe fell under a deluge of syphilis outbreaks in the late sixteenth century. Unattractive hair loss was a classic symptom of this venereal disease, along with sores, fever, and body aches. But the hair loss was the most abhorred symptom, since a full head of healthy hair was an important marker of virulent health and wealth [1]. What did the hapless men who contracted syphilis do? Those sickened with the disease concealed their revolting symptoms in the most unthinkable way: they wore lush, decadent wigs.

Wigmakers fashioned fancy wigs for the elite using goat hair, horse hair, or sometimes human hair [1]. The barely tamed mesh of long locks and loose curls beautifully hid the ugly lesions on the faces of the men who'd become stricken with illness.

It wasn't long before France's King Louis XIII joined the club of men wearing a periwig. He was a mere seventeen-year-old lad when his hair began to fall out in patches, with some historians assuming he fell into the unlucky lot of people who'd caught syphilis

[1]. He was a king, and as a young man who gave orders from the velvet seat of his imperial throne, he had to look the part. Patchy baldness was not a becoming look for a member of the royal family. What was he to do? The most obvious thing, of course: hire forty-eight wigmakers to produce one fab wig fit for a king [1]. And a trend was born.

King Louis XIII confidently sported his dark, flowing wig of flamboyant curls during public appearances. Aristocrats wanted a piece of the king's swagger and commissioned their own wigmakers to handcraft silken hairpieces fit for noblemen. Eventually, the upper-middle classes also began wearing wigs fit for seventeenth-century France's bourgeoisie. Wearing a periwig became a symbol of elegance, power, and sophistication throughout all of Europe [2].

Wigs were fashioned in all colors, in all lengths, and with the precise level of defying curl a customer desired. Any color a horse came in, whether black or red or brown, a wig in that color could be instantly woven. Sunny blonde locks and silvery hair were in high demand [2]. Of all hairstyles, naturally curly hair was the holy grail. Those who couldn't afford to pay a premium for natural curls settled for straight hair, which could be artificially curled [2]. Women often sold their locks to hair collectors for a tidy sum [2]. The European periwig industry flourished, with everyday wigs selling for a week's worth of pay and more extravagant ones for the price of over half a year's income [1].

While donning a periwig lent gentlemen a level of sophistication they couldn't otherwise naturally express, the hairpieces delivered their own extreme set of drawbacks. Delicately woven, wigs couldn't be handwashed at home in a basin full of sudsy bathwater. Personal hygiene wasn't a priority either in the sixteenth and seventeenth centuries, so why would anyone bother washing a wig worn directly over an oily scalp for several hours during a sweltering summer day? Naturally, periwigs gave off not only a welcoming air of elegance but a repugnant whiff of intolerable grossness.

Unsurprisingly, those donning periwigs kept smelling bottles on hand like they were First Aid kits. Men pampered their wigs with fragrances, ranging from lavender to rose petal and cinnamon [2]. A putrid odor wasn't the only issue. Lice and fleas built cozy nests inside the periwigs, considering they offered an ample supply of organic food just a few millimeters away, at the scalp. The pomade used to set the periwigs was produced from animal fat, which grew rancid over time and served as an appetizing, three-course feast for pesky fleas [2]. Powdering wigs was thought to be quite the elegant thing to do to freshen up their obnoxious scent. The powder consisted of a fine blend of chalk plus corn or bean flour [2]. As would be expected, European bourgeoisie politely excused themselves to go off and powder their periwigs in the most discreet, gentlemanly fashion.

Men gifted with intelligence and precocious talents donned the periwig. Composers, from Bach to Handel, as well as aristocrats, courtiers, and anyone who could tolerate the unpleasant odors emanating from a heavily used periwig felt obliged to wear one. The periwig fad endured until people's nasal congestion cleared up in the late eighteenth century. Hair powder was also taxed in 1795, economically wiping out a sizeable portion of wig wearers in Britain [1]. A more natural look took over in Europe, and the era of flaunting poufy periwigs had phased out.

Wearing a periwig was not an entirely bad idea. Who wouldn't jump at the chance to give their neck and back muscles a strenuous workout by hanging an elaborate periwig over the top of their head for several hours straight? Aside from helping to improve posture, periwigs reduced the risk of people catching lice. Instead of latching directly onto the hair, the unsuspecting lice were fooled into taking shelter in the deep caverns of the periwig itself [1]. And voila! Painful lice infestations were skillfully averted.

Now, what the fashionable men of the sixteenth and seventeenth centuries needed was a modern convenience to keep those periwigs clean and in good condition. Only the remarkable and versatile baking soda could've done the job. Baking soda is a natural deodorizer, absorbing smells like a vacuum picking up dust balls. A baking soda bath would've done wonders for the cleanliness of an aristocrat's dainty periwig. All a gentleman had to do was to collect water in a bucket, add a handful of baking soda, and carefully soak the periwig for five minutes to remove the entirety of loathsome odors.

As an alternative to the forbidden wash, a dry sprinkle of baking soda into the periwig would've served as an equally powerful odor-remover. And cleaning up the periwig wouldn't have been the only trick up baking soda's sleeve. Sodium bicarbonate would've also reduced the unnatural shine on a periwig and given it a soft, bouncy feel. A fresh-smelling, bouncy wig would've been a welcome alternative to the foul reality experienced by gents donning the popular periwig.

But baking soda is a truly modern convenience, invented only as recently as 1801—when the trend of wearing a delicate mop of curls on one's head had already faded into distant history. Pharmacist Valentin Rose the Younger discovered sodium bicarbonate. Naturally, he hadn't intended for it to be used specifically for cleaning periwigs, whose time had passed. Baking soda was perfectly suited for several other uses, though, such as serving as an effective fire extinguisher, acid neutralizer, sports supplement, medical treatment, and of course, a disinfectant [3].

This modern convenience arrived far too late to be of use to the sixteenth and seventeenth century kings, aristocrats, and bourgeoisie. Baking soda's late arrival wouldn't have mattered, since almost no one prioritized personal hygiene back then anyhow.

13

IVAN THE TERRIBLE AND POWER RECLINERS

Ivan IV earned his fitting nickname, Ivan the Terrible, for spreading a reign of terror throughout Russia. Proclaimed the first tsar of Russia in 1547, Ivan was nothing short of, indeed, terrible. His moniker was far from a form of flattery, despite the word "terrible" being interpreted as "awe-inspiring" by sixteenth century commoners [1]. Rather, Ivan the Terrible inspired nonstop fear over his squeamish subjects high in the hills and low in the valleys—essentially everywhere.

Ivan was proclaimed grand prince of Moscow at the tender age of three, when his father suddenly passed away. His mother ruled on his behalf, but only until he was eight years old, when she, too, died, likely from being poisoned. A helpless orphan, Ivan became the center of vicious struggles for power between conflicting factions of nobles, whom he learned to mistrust and despise for the rest of his life [1, 2].

As an orphaned lad in Moscow, Ivan and his brother were raised in conditions that would hardly befit a grand prince. Often starving and dressed in rags, Ivan felt he and his brother were treated like common vagrants by the nobles [1]. Power hungry, these nobles callously toyed with Ivan in attempts to seize ultimate control. A growing hatred took seat in the heart of the young man, and he expressed his unhealthy bitterness by cruelly throwing helpless animals out of windows [1].

Crowned tsar and grand prince of all of Russia as a lanky teenager, the seventeen-year-old Ivan held complete power. Administration reforms and reorganizations took place during his early years as emperor [2]. He drew up an updated legal code to replace the one that had been languishing for fifty years [2]. He revamped the military, appointing commanders on the basis of meritorious effort rather than noble birth [2]. He aimed to reduce the powers inherited by the nobles, a clear act of vindication for the neglect he suffered at their hands as a boy. Printing presses were first introduced into Russia thanks to Ivan [1].

Ivan's peaceful first years as emperor disappeared into oblivion as a result of two major events that dramatically shook him and distorted his worldview. The first was the death of his adored wife, Anastasia, whom he'd married a month after being crowned emperor of Russia [2]. Enraged and full of sorrow, he suspected she'd been poisoned by his ruthless enemies [1]. It wasn't until 400 years later that her bones were exhumed and fatal amounts of mercury were discovered in them—perhaps proving Ivan's suspicions [1].

The second event that unsettled Ivan's already-unstable world was the defection of his field commander and friend, Prince Kurbsky, during the Livonian War [2]. Ivan contemplated abdicating because of his hurtful act of betrayal. Ivan was convinced to remain in power, but only on the condition that he could deal with traitors as he wished—which meant outright execution [2]. Anywhere from one to 6,000 men formed the *oprichniki*, which held the authority to unleash unhinged terror on anyone outside of Ivan's immediate circle [2].

Dressed from head to toe in black, the menacing *oprichniki* was occasionally led by Ivan himself [2]. They served as his personal bodyguards, enforcing the laws in Ivan's newly created territory [2]. Torture and on-the-spot executions were warranted for anyone who dared to betray the emperor again. A violent fate awaited

Russians who were even alleged to show disloyalty. In 1570, Ivan led the *oprichniki* in Novogorod, brutally killing several thousand of the city's inhabitants [2].

The waves of cruelties and murders carried out by the *oprichniki* lasted for seven long years until it was finally abolished [2]. But Ivan had already cemented his reputation for being a bloodthirsty savage and an unstable ruler. His reputation only worsened in his later years when he kicked his pregnant daughter-in-law so brutally that she miscarried. When his son—and only viable heir—learned the fate of his unborn child, he confronted Ivan, only to receive a violent blow to the head. A few days later, Ivan's son died of his injury. Russia's Time of Troubles, a period overcome with political crises, was ushered in [2].

Ivan the Terrible may have been terrible, but he was needlessly so. As the first tsar of Russia, he sat on a magnificent gilded throne designed to inspire fear and awe in anyone who dared set eyes on the ruler. But this throne, built from wood and overlaid with gold, would've been highly uncomfortable to sit upon for any duration of time [3]. How cozy could it have been to sit on a rigid block of gilded wood? No matter how many opulent cushions his court subjects tucked into the seat of the throne, it wouldn't have been comfortable. It's no wonder Ivan the Terrible was constantly angry. With a stone-hard throne to sit upon, who wouldn't have been?

Now, had Ivan the Terrible only had access to a modern convenience—the power recliner—perhaps his fury might have been taken down a degree, or several. By sitting back in the cozy seat of a power recliner, built with the ability to give soothing massages, Ivan the Terrible would've been a calm, comfortable, and likable emperor with a heart of gold. His stylish power recliner would've fit perfectly with the aesthetics of the palace, manufactured specifically for royalty. It would've had an imperial leather look suited for the sixteenth century ruler and even offered a swivel feature, so that Ivan the Terrible could've gazed tranquilly on the dastardly nobles standing with a slight quiver before him. As the only recliner in the court, it would've given Ivan the Terrible plenty of space to recline to the max. He wouldn't have even had to wait for delivery, because the cushiony throne would've been built a short walk from the emperor's palace. Plus, with an easy gliding motion, the recliner could've been manipulated to seamlessly move forward and backward, thereby transporting Ivan the Terrible into a welcome state of relaxation.

If only Ivan the Terrible had access to the power recliner, he might not have earned himself an unflattering nickname that's followed him for nearly half a millennium. Instead, he might've been known as Ivan the Tranquil. He'd have dealt with the quarrelling, disruptive nobles with a peaceful air. Instead of dispatching the *oprichniki*, as Ivan the Tranquil, he'd have let loose an army of men who'd have been responsible for facilitating the daily comfort of Russia's ordinary citizens, perhaps building them versions of a recliner fit for the average commoner. How revered Ivan the Tranquil would've been!

But the initial design of today's recliners didn't appear until the twentieth century—400 years after Ivan the Terrible had the gall to unleash a reign of murderous destruction on innocent citizens. Undoubtedly, the power recliner would've given a level of ease to Ivan the Terrible, and precluded a reign that was washed in blood, where almost no one lived to tell the tale.

14

MOZART AND JOKE-A-DAY APPS

No musical composer in the history of Western music has been as versatile, prolific, and mischievous as Johann Chrysostom Wolfgang Amadeus Mozart, known fondly to music lovers as Mozart. Unbeknownst to the music world at the time of his birth in Salzburg, Austria, in 1756, the Classical period would soon ascend to new and glorious heights.

Mozart was a prodigious composer, having tried his hand at composing concertos from the age of five [1]. He began performing at the Bavarian court, then Viennese noble houses and imperial courts [1]. A family tour with his father and sister soon followed, and western Europe—from Munich to Frankfurt and Brussels, then Paris and London—was introduced to the musical genius who'd become one of the world's most recognizable composers [1].

His nimble intellect picked up the nuances of musical compositions and retained them. At age fourteen, for instance, Mozart listened to Gregorio Allegri's *Miserere* while he visited Rome during Holy Week [1, 2]. Upon returning later that day, he wrote down the entire composition strictly from memory [1].

As he matured musically, Mozart composed several symphonies, a handful of divertimentos, and numerous sacred works [1]. He wrote comic operas, such as *The Feigned Gardener Girl,* in his playful, lighthearted signature style, which was met with much fanfare [1]. Concertos, more divertimentos, and serenades followed [1]. The gifted Mozart achieved a lifetime of triumphs before having turned twenty-one. He was still traveling throughout Europe, all while exchanging letters with his family.

Yet even as Mozart matured professionally, his sense of humor remained charmingly infantile. Letters he penned to his cousin, Maria Anna Thekla, were filled with obscene jokes [1]. Toilet humor tickled not only Mozart's fancy but that of his entire family. Mozart never missed a chance to include in his correspondence risqué comedy about universal human embarrassments, from constipation to urination and flatulence.

His crude sense of humor spilled over into his compositions. In 1782 in Vienna, Mozart wrote a set of canons, one of which included the canon in B-flat major, *Leck mich im Arsch*, which literally translated to English from German as *Lick me in the Arse* [3, 4]. Six daring voices would've sung this lively and irreverent party piece Mozart wrote for his boisterous, likeminded friends [4]. Unsurprisingly, Mozart's publisher didn't appreciate his indiscreet humor and revised the text to *Let us be glad!* [4].

Mozart didn't stop at composing at just one explicit canon. *Bona Nox, K. 561*, was his canon in A major, and written for four voices [5]. A pianist would've lightly run his lithe fingers over the ivory piano keys as the bombastic lyrics were sung a cappella, to the shock of prim and proper audiences. Mozart was credited with writing the lyrics, which started with a decorous "goodnight" in Latin, Italian, French, and English, then ended with the miscreant lyrics, "Shit in your bed and make it burst . . ." [5]. It was the rare few who managed to resist Mozart's impish sense of humor set to effervescent music.

One or two obscene compositions, though, couldn't satisfy a prolific musical prodigy like Mozart, who sought to devise as many playful lyrics and musical pieces as possible. *Difficile Lectu, K. 559*, Mozart's canon in F major for three singers, was completed around

1787 [6]. The canon was punctuated with a series of bilingual puns that, when sung, were heard as vulgar German and Italian phrases [6]. Mozart composed this piece for his friend, baritone Johann Nepomuk Peyerl, who sang with a such a thick Bavarian accent that it caused particular Latin lyrics to sound like lewd German ones [3, 6]. Like all of Mozart's music—the proper ones included—*Difficile Lectu* was a ball of fun for anyone open-minded enough to listen.

Since the dawn of civilization, toilet humor has remained popular with the common crowds—and Mozart was no exception. His vast range included masterful, sprightly music occasionally paired with deviant lyrics. Who'd ever expect a main course of musical virtuoso to be served with a whimsical side of vulgar lyrics? The aural irony was without parallel, but unerringly delightful.

Now, what Mozart might have appreciated to enhance his bawdy revelry was a modern convenience—the joke-a-day app. He'd have chuckled every morning as he read the daily one-liners on his phone. With one tap, he'd have easily sent the jokes to his mother, father, and cousin back home, inspiring hearty laughs across his whole family. The joke-a-day app would've brightened Mozart's long journeys across western Europe, through gloomy London, and upon returning home to Salzburg. Given Mozart's mischievous personality, he'd have invited the stagecoach driver into the fun, and the entire ride would've been as unforgettable as his music.

With the right app, he could've starred his all-time favorite jokes for quick availability at opportune moments. Aside from composing *A Little Night Music*, there'd have been nothing more satisfying for Mozart than telling a crude joke and eliciting that precious grunt and roll of the eyes. Mozart's app would've offered him the opportunity to choose from a wide range of topics, and he would've zeroed in on the lewdest jokes that promised to deliver the heartiest laughs. What an incredible asset the joke-of-the-day app would've been to Mozart, who would've fit the hilarious one-liners into his busy life of composing over 800 musical works, enchanting audiences and enlivening social merrymaking all over Europe.

But apps only rose to popularity in the twenty-first century—around 200 years after the time Mozart composed his most comical and playful operas, like the *Marriage of Figaro* in 1786. Considering his wily sense of humor, Mozart would've immediately downloaded the most well-rated joke-a-day app. And it wouldn't have cost him a thing—except to contribute to his winsome reputation for reveling in the naughtiest of contemporary jokes.

15

VIKINGS AND SMART SHOWERS

Known in the long annals of history as the most barbaric of warriors, the Vikings had rightfully earned their fierce reputation at sea. Beginning in 793 C.E., brutal Norsemen warred with peaceful monks on the northeast coast of England, then battled viciously along the pastures of Scotland, ripped up towns in nearby Ireland, and made their belligerent presence known in France [1]. The resulting influence of the Danish, Swedish, and Norwegian warriors ran deep.

Their Scandinavian languages mixed with English, ensuring the days of the week, Thursday and Friday, were named after the Nordic deities Thor and Frigg, respectively. Since their first invasion until the end of the Viking Age in 1066 C.E. and beyond, Viking DNA mingled with the populations of conquered lands.

Terrorizing helpless citizens in faraway nations to compensate for the overpopulation in their homelands was all in a day's work [2]. But despite brutally conquering innocent people and seizing Europe's coastal cities, the formidable Vikings weren't always the raiding kind. In fact, when the Norse explorers weren't sailing their longships and plundering villages, they lived peaceably among themselves, farming land. Agriculture flourished in 800 C.E., with the Danes cultivating rye, barley, and wheat as well as raising cows, pigs, and sheep on self-sufficient farms [3]. They lived an idyllic, pastoral life.

Unarmed Viking men and women were quite an admirable sort—so esteemed, in fact, that they had gained the reputation for being the cleanest people in all of Europe during the largely unhygienic Middle Ages. Bathing was indeed a priority for every Viking man and woman. Each Saturday was reserved especially for this purifying act of personal hygiene, referred to reverently as "bathing day" [4]. A combination of water heated at home and handmade soap kept Vikings cleaner than anyone else in Europe.

When not participating in a terrifying raid, the Vikings bathed on Saturdays after a hearty supper of meat, grains, fruits, and vegetables. In winter, the resourceful Danes piped water into their homes for their leisurely baths [4]. In summer, they took pleasurable dips under waterfalls or in fresh-water streams [4]. With its position between two tectonic plates, Iceland gave Vikings a delightful opportunity to take cleansing baths in its countless hot springs [4]. Vikings combined animal fats and processed wood ash to make a sudsy soap [5]. This lye soap was valued for its ability to eliminate head lice as well as bleach the Vikings' beards and hair a highly desirable California blond.

While the Vikings had it together when it came to cleanliness, one modern convenience would have enhanced their hygiene routines significantly—the smart shower. Surely, geothermal hot springs would have been amazing places to bathe. But water temperatures inside an Icelandic hot spring could potentially rise to 111 degrees Fahrenheit, making bathing more like boiling.

But smart showers in the Viking Age would've given the Danes a highly personalized and consistently comfortable bath experience. The Nordic men and women would have simply had to set the water temperature to a precise ninety-eight degrees, switch on their lighting preferences, adjust the water flow, and perhaps add sound to maximize their enjoyment. Plus, all this could've been conveniently done via voice command. Vikings making use of a smart shower would've no longer had to risk being dangerously scalded by hot springs heated by erratic underground volcanic activity. No more languishing for several long minutes while the kettle slowly heated the water at home, because smart showers could've been started with a voice command while the Vikings relished their meat and potatoes. By the time they'd consumed their Saturday supper, the bath would've been warm and ready.

As the Vikings prized warfare, a fallen warrior was buried with his sword, shield, and the daily essentials believed to guarantee his welfare in the next world. A wealthy Viking was also ceremoniously buried, but in his impressive wooden longship, one cleverly built to sail forward and back from the sandy shores. Regardless, Vikings were respectfully buried with the valuables they cherished most, whether that was a favorite sword used on the battlefield, a fine-tooth comb exquisitely carved from reindeer antlers—or, had this modern convenience been around, the shiny components of a smart shower. The Vikings would've showed immense veneration for a technology that would've given them the practical means to practice excellent hygiene on a daily basis and in the eternal afterlife.

16

REMBRANDT AND THE SELFIE STICK

No Dutch painter's portraits have ever been as emotionally evocative as those of Rembrandt Harmenszoon van Rijn. Familiar to art lovers only as Rembrandt, his paintings strayed from meager simplicity and dove into expressions of profound, complex emotions—rare qualities that made his works of art highly desirable by wealthy art collectors of his day.

While Rembrandt's portrait commissions earned him enough wealth to purchase a lavish home in Amsterdam, his self-portraits gave him international name and fame. As a young student, Rembrandt interpreted mythological stories and captured them on the blank canvas [1]. In doing so, he painted himself as a bystander, or onlooker, within the compositions. These early paintings fueled his lifelong obsession with self-portraiture [1].

Over the length and breadth of his distinguished career, Rembrandt painted eighty or so self-portraits. Starting at age twenty-two, when he sported dewy skin and plump features, and continuing until he was sixty-three and worn under sagging cheeks and tired eyes, Rembrandt painted fifty paintings, thirty etches, and nearly ten drawings of himself [2]. He was a prolific master of his art.

One of his earliest self-portraits may have been his "Self Portrait at an Early Age," painted in 1629. The distant look in his eyes remained hidden beneath dark shadows, and the loose ends of his tousled auburn hair playfully caught the paltry light source behind him. His intention behind this inventive first self-portrait may have been to experiment with various lighting effects [3].

A year later, in 1630, Rembrandt created an etching known as "Self Portrait in a Cap, Open-Mouthed." In this alluring etching, Rembrandt was a budding, mustached twenty-four-year-old. Using quick strokes, he convincingly re-created the emotion of pleasant surprise, leaving the onlooker immediately charmed and struck by his genius.

That same year, the style of his self-portraiture matured. He appeared contemplative in his "Self Portrait," dressed elegantly in a dark cloak and fashionable felt hat. His furrowed brows and slightly pursed lips reveal a thoughtful, tranquil demeanor.

Within ten years, his style dramatically changed. No longer the carefree young adult, but a professional artist aiming to equate himself in status with the affluent sitters he painted, Rembrandt put oil and brush to canvas and produced "Self Portrait at the Age of 34" in 1640 [4]. Like all his self-portraits, Rembrandt peered out with a steadfast gaze, showing complete recognition of his exemplary inborn artistic gifts.

And in 1660, toward the end of his life, Rembrandt depicted himself on canvas as a wise and insightful aged man, weary of life, yet mustering onward. The wrinkles on his forehead were pronounced, perhaps deepened by the tragic losses of his beloved first wife and child and his severe financial setbacks. The expression on his face was one of, "So this has been my life!" The colors were rich and dark, showcasing the artist's prevailing talent despite his life's fluctuating fortunes.

Throughout his life, Rembrandt never swayed from painting self-portraits. His reasons for embarking on his quest to capture himself at every stage of life varied. Some self-portraits were painted to show clients what they could expect if they sat for him. Painting self-portraits also gave him plenty of practice [3]. After all, he had a reliable and affordable model in himself. Experimenting with lighting, mood, and costumes also gave Rembrandt sufficient reasons to engage in a series of self-portraits over the course of his life. By pondering the exquisiteness of his work, it's unsurprising that the Dutch painter's self-portraits remained in high demand.

But one persistent endeavor, especially during his early professional life, was capturing the breadth of his emotions. Fear, anger, sadness, laughter, and happiness lived variously on his face [3]. Rembrandt practiced his art, while studying the different attitudes reflected on a sitter's face. To perfect his technique, he'd paint himself in different moods.

Now, had Rembrandt only had access to today's the selfie stick, he'd have been able to capture his naturally varying moods instantly and single-handedly. Since artists relied on visual reference to develop a realistic work of art, it would have been expedient for Rembrandt to carry around a selfie stick with an attached smartphone, using it whenever an alternate mood presented itself. As emotions are transitory, the expediency would have been invaluable.

Anger, for instance, dissipates within twenty minutes in the average person. Without the capability to take a selfie right away, Rembrandt would have had to rush his artistic process in a fit of rage, in order to accurately depict this emotion. And succumbing to anger of any degree is a major hurdle in performing a serious endeavor with quality. By taking a selfie with the convenient selfie stick, however, the artist would've had instant and long-lasting access to the scowl on his face, thereby allowing him to paint from this valuable point of reference—the selfie photo.

Today, people laugh for an average of five minutes per day (much less than the nearly twenty minutes in ages past). Rembrandt showed an interest in how laughing changed the appearance of the face [3]. How handy it would have been for him to snap a selfie during a hearty laugh, then recreate his squinched eyes, his open mouth displaying a full front set of teeth, and his bowled-over look as the he held his tummy in joyous agony. Painting from a candid selfie would have given him the observational ability to notice the fine details of the human form that he may have never had the chance to scrutinize before, without making his sitters uncomfortable.

Happiness persists for the short span of three days before an individual returns to their baseline emotional state. An experienced painter could've created a portrait in a little over half a day, but the amount of time for completion varied in accordance with the complexity of the painting. Some portraits took months before the painter was satisfied and the work was finished. In no way could exuberant happiness be sustained for such lengthy periods. But having a selfie stick on hand to capture the fleeting moments of joy would've given Rembrandt enough time to study the photo and, at leisure, paint his self-portrait with a high degree of likeness, for which he consistently strived throughout his career [2].

Indeed, the renowned painter would have appreciated the continual supply of diverse facial expressions from which he could sort through and brilliantly bring to life on canvas. Art collectors of his day would've praised his work in portraiture even more than they did. By being able to perfectly depict the slightest nuances of his own emotions, his expert skill would have enhanced the many portraits commissioned by his wealthy sitters, thereby earning him considerably more than enough riches to pay off the creditors chasing him, and preventing his financial ruin.

But the modern selfie stick was only invented in 2005, over 300 years after Rembrandt painted one of his last self-portraits, the "Self Portrait at the Age of 63." Rembrandt's genius for realizing the subtleties of human expressions was only quadrupled by the fact that he didn't have an opportunity to seize the artistic benefits this modern technology might have afforded him. If he lived today, he'd have strolled the quaint streets of the Netherlands with a selfie stick tucked into his backpack, ready to be used at any opportune moment.

Fortunately for today's portrait painters, the selfie stick has the capability to capture ephemeral feelings and serve as a reference while artists paint any of the vast ranges of human emotion—those Rembrandt himself would have willingly paid a dear price to preserve.

17

WEI KING PHYSICIAN HUA TUO AND IBUPROFEN

Throbbing head pain has long afflicted significant portions of humanity. Whether due to head trauma or chemical, nerve, or neurological activity, effective and permanent headache remedies have escaped humans since the dawn of civilization.

But early innovative medical practitioners sought to quell the pain of headaches at their source: the skull. Trepanation, as the procedure was known, involved boring two-to-three-inch-wide holes into the skull of an individual, relieving pressure in the brain and providing therapeutic relief [1]. Given that modern anesthesia hadn't been developed until the twentieth century, pain from the procedure was intolerable. Naturally, any form of primitive surgery on the scalp would have potentially caused substantially more pain than the headache itself. Nevertheless, according to archaeological evidence from numerous ancient cultures and geographic locations, trepanation wasn't uncommon.

Trephined skulls, in fact, have been found all over the globe, from Peru to France and Israel [1]. Archaeologists unearthed a significant number of trephined skulls in China too. The time periods are equally revealing: trephined skulls have been linked to the late Paleolithic period, between 40,000 and 10,000 years ago, all the way to the Renaissance in Italy, which began in the fourteenth century and ended in the early seventeenth [1].

Boring holes in the skull was achieved with tools, such as obsidian, flint, and metal knives [1]. In Renaissance Italy, using flint to scrape the hard skull could take a medical practitioner almost an hour. The skull could also be cut, after which the disc of bone was lifted out [1]. Using a trephine, a device consisting of a hollow cylinder with a sharp, jagged edge, was the preferred method in the time of Hippocrates in the fifth century B.C.E. [1]. In the Middle Ages, a drill and chisel were favored tools for trepanation [1]. Ancient Peruvians similarly drilled several concentric holes in a patient's skull, then chiseled out the bone between the holes [1]. Unbelievably, patients who underwent trepanation survived for days, months, or years after the surgery [1].

During the time of Hippocrates, trepanation was useful as a remedy for head injuries. Bleeding inside the head was thought to cause stagnant blood, which could've turned into an unwanted case of pus. Letting out the blood in the head before it had a chance to decay was believed to be the most optimal course of treatment, suitable for the likes of Greek soldiers wounded in war [1]. In ancient China, trepanation was the go-to solution for severe headaches.

In fact, in early third century China, trepanation was advocated by eminent doctors, like Hua Tuo [2]. The Chinese physician and surgeon won fame for his successes in surgical procedures, such as partial splenectomies and laparotomies, as well as herbal anesthetics made from hemp [3]. Well-traveled and well-read, Hua Tuo took Chinese surgery to new heights, but his journey toward his professional zenith was cut dramatically short [3].

Hua Tuo's surgical accomplishments earned him appointment to the emperor's court. He was given the position of court physician to the Wei king, Cao Cao [3]. The Wei dynasty was one of northern China's most powerful and enduring dynasties before its unification in later periods. Cao Cao was on par with the notable Chinese warlords of his day.

Crafty and brilliant, the genius warlord began his military career at the tender age of twenty, soon serving as the grand chancellor [4]. Cao Cao conquered the Yan Province, battled the Zhong dynasty emperor Yuan Shu, and claimed victory in the Battle of Rangcheng [4]. Over a series of conquests, Cao Cao, at the age of fifty-eight, was awarded ten cities, which became known as Wei [4]. Four years later, his status was elevated to King of Wei, and he served as its vassal king [4]. Cao Cao wasn't officially the Emperor Wu of Wei during his lifetime; rather, his son bestowed the title upon him posthumously [4].

Cao Cao—who'd fought countless bloody battles, conquered vast territories, and subdued vilified enemy emperors—exhibited some tyrannical tendencies. As a warlord experienced on the battlefront, it was inevitable that he'd endure several painful wounds while engaged in vicious conflict. It was this vassal king who, at the age of sixty-five, developed intolerable head pain. Clearly, he could withstand serious physical battlefield wounds—but a throbbing headache was something he could not endure. Cao Cao summoned his court physician, Hua Tuo, for immediate relief.

Hua Tuo promptly arrived at Cao Cao's bedside and stood before his superior. The physician carefully examined the king, taking his pulse and offering temporary relief with acupuncture [3]. He then diagnosed a tumor and recommended a swift remedy: trepanation [3]. Hua Tuo could permanently resolve the king's headache by drilling a hole in his head. Being experienced in anesthetizing patients with concoctions made from hemp, Hua Tuo could've performed the procedure while causing minimal pain to the ailing Cao Cao. In ancient China, however, a perfect success rate was unlikely. After all, a craniotomy in the third century was nothing short of crude, and risks for infection were high [2].

Upon hearing that Hua Tuo intended to drill a hole or two into his skull, Cao Cao believed that his enemies had bribed the distinguished Chinese physician to kill him [3]. Convinced by the waywardness of his imagination, Cao Cao flew into a rage, condemning

Hua Tuo to prison and execution [3]. Such was how Hua Tuo, the most renowned Chinese surgeon, met his untimely end. Doubling the misfortune between the walls of the Wei palace, Cao Cao himself died shortly thereafter from the malady responsible for his head pain.

Now, had Hua Tuo only had access to a modern convenience—ibuprofen—he'd have fared much better, especially in terms of longevity. When summoned to Cao Cao's side, the court physician, instead of suggesting trepanation, could have confidently prescribed ibuprofen. Upon providing the king with a dose of the popular non-steroidal anti-inflammatory drug, Hua Tuo would have relieved the headache caused by inflammation from Cao Cao's tumor—and saved his own dear life in the process. Offering a couple of pain relievers would've been far less intrusive and risky than drilling two holes into the king's skull and rhythmically chipping away sections of it.

But ibuprofen wasn't invented until 1961, nearly 2,000 years after the era of China's greatest physician, Hua Tuo. Dr. Stewart Adams, O.B.E., was the scientist credited with the discovery [6]. He and John Nicholson, an organic chemist, patented the drug in 1961. Subsequently, ibuprofen became one of the world's most preferred and effective pain relievers.

Ibuprofen is so effective in relieving headaches that one-quarter of headache sufferers experience relief within two hours after taking the recommended dose of 400 mg [7]. Tension headaches are quickly relieved with ibuprofen, allowing people to once again concentrate and work. And ibuprofen doesn't require a prescription; a bottle can be conveniently purchased over the counter.

Had ibuprofen been around nearly 2,000 years ago, Cao Cao would've ordered a member of his court to obtain a bottle from the local market. A prescription from Hua Tuo would've been unnecessary. Within two hours of taking a dose of ibuprofen, Cao Cao's headache would've disappeared, and he'd have avoided expressing his unbridled fury toward his court physician. Most importantly, the innocent Hua Tuo would never have been unjustly thrown into prison and executed ten days later. The distinguished father of Chinese medicine would've gone on for many more years to widen his depth and breadth of Chinese medicinal knowledge.

Hua Tuo's book of medical writings, *Book of the Blue Bag*, would have survived and contributed to the growth of medicine, instead of being tossed into a fire and lost for all perpetuity. Fortunately, today's royals and commoners alike experience relief from throbbing headaches every day because of this priceless, universal wonder drug.

18

GEORGE WASHINGTON AND DENTAL IMPLANTS

In 1789, the Electoral College unanimously elected George Washington as President of the United States. Winning the first presidency of the fledgling nation was an admirable feat. Despite his distinguished status, Washington couldn't shake his poor oral health. Since his twenties, he'd been afflicted with ongoing tooth decay, inevitable tooth loss, and agonizing toothaches [1].

Upon taking the oath of office during his inauguration, President Washington had only one natural tooth left in his mouth—a hardy premolar [1, 3]. A set of crude dentures improved his ability to utter the famous words reserved for none other than those eminent few who held the office of the US president: "I do solemnly swear that I will faithfully execute the Office of President of the United States, and will to the best of my ability, preserve, protect, and defend the Constitution of the United States." A lack of dentures would have made it impossible to pronounce this single poignant sentence with dignity and without great difficulty.

Furthermore, as a testament to his admirable commitment to selflessly serving the nation, President Washington made the choice to give the first presidential inaugural address—an act not required by the Constitution [2]. A crowd numbering in the hundreds, including prominent members of Congress, troops, and local citizens, stood under the balcony of Federal Hall to hear the President's speech [2]. What an unforgettable speech it was, especially with its grand follow-up of evening fireworks.

He started his inaugural speech with, "Fellow citizens of the Senate and the House of Representatives: Among the vicissitudes incident to life, no event could have filled me with greater anxieties . . ." Undoubtedly, as the first president, George Washington felt trepidation, but even more so by admitting he'd inherited "inferior endowments from nature . . ." Clearly, he was referencing his poor dental health.

Fortunately for George Washington, he wore presidential dentures—a set that gave him reasonable ability to ensure his words were comprehensible. In fact, he had several dentures over the course of his lifetime of sixty-seven years. His specially made dentures were assembled with hippopotamus ivory, or ivory from a walrus or elephant [1]. A few of his dentures partially consisted of cow or horse teeth. And we all know how valuable a strong set of quarter-inch to two-inch cow teeth can be for grinding tough food and shredding it to digestible pieces.

New Yorker Dr. Joh Greenwood, George Washington's dentist and friend, assembled a set of dentures regarded as quite advanced for the time [1]. Carved hippopotamus ivory, held together by gold wire springs and brass screws, were combined with human teeth [1]. The expert dentist even left a hole in the set to make room for his patient's single remaining natural tooth [1]. Of course, in time, due to poor diet and diseases of the era, George Washington's only tooth also fell out.

Regardless, the President complained of oral pain even from Greenwood's well-crafted dentures [1]. He acquired a bulging lip, seen today in his portrait on the front of the US dollar bill. And, contrary to popular myth, George Washington never wore wooden dentures—no one of his time did. His dentures resembled wood only because of the food and beverage stains that darkened the ivory or bone components an unsightly brown [3].

George Washington partied—and his favorite drink was Madeira wine, produced on the Madeira Islands off the coast of Africa [3]. He savored the smooth and complex flavors of this fortified wine, enjoying the dry varieties during elegant parties, before dinners, or between meals. Squeezed from red or white grapes, the full-bodied Madeira wine was deliberately oxidized and heated, resulting in its amber color. As President Washington sipped his favorite wine, he irreparably stained his ivory dentures. The "wooden look" developed as the dark liquid seeped into the tiny fractures in the bone, but not the rest of the teeth, thereby creating a look that resembled wood grains [3].

Now, had the eighteenth century only been blessed with advanced dental technology, George Washington wouldn't have suffered such grave discomfort and pain from his dentures. Today's dental implants would have given the nation's first president a great deal of confidence, and a life without chronic mouth pain. With the help of modern dental implants, he'd have effortlessly spoken the humble words of his great presidential inaugural address before throngs of citizens proud to be led by his political dexterity and moral integrity.

But modern-day dental implants were only first fitted into human patients in 1965, slightly less than 200 years after George Washington won the office of the presidency. Although crude forms of dental implants, carved from bamboo, were implanted into human mouths since 2000 B.C.E., they were no match for the comfort and ease produced by today's dental implants—which remain barely noticeable to the wearer fortunate enough to be able to afford a complete set. Dental implants enhanced quality of life by facilitating the wearer's natural ability to once again chew, talk, and flash a thousand-watt smile. Had George Washington only had access to this modern convenience, we'd enjoy portraits of him wearing a full-toothed grin—a delight we're forever denied, because of his ill-fitting dental apparatuses.

Today's dental implants are permanent fixtures, unlike dentures that popped out intentionally or accidentally, depending on the occasion. Surely, George Washington's dentures, made of brass and other metals, would have been too clunky and heavy to tolerate comfortably. It's no wonder he appeared mum in all his portraits. It'd have taken immense effort to navigate speaking, chewing, and smiling with a mouth full of metal, while withstanding the nagging possibility that a screw could, at any time, loosen and unexpectedly pierce his tender cheek. Nevertheless, George Washington handled wearing dentures with grace and poise, just as he did in leading the entire nation.

19

BLACKBEARD AND ELECTRIC SHAVERS

The Golden Age of Piracy was rife with looting, trash-talking, unshaven pirates who waited for the command to attack and seize merchant ships laden heavily with valuables. One of the most well-known of pirates was Edward Teach, better known as Blackbeard. While his illegal pursuits were well-known, the English pirate, in many ways, remained shrouded in uncertainty.

He could've been born in Bristol, England in 1680, or perhaps New York or Denmark [1]. Regardless of his country of birth, the sea called to him at an early age. In the War of Spanish Successions, Blackbeard served as a privateer [1]. These professionals were granted the legal authority to plunder ships of rival nations. At times, these commissions would go beyond what a king or queen sanctioned, blurring the boundary separating privateer from pirate [2].

Blackbeard, however, launched his full-blown pirate career in 1713 [3]. In order to carry out his new role with all the bells and whistles fit for a daring maritime pirate, he cultivated a peculiar personal image. He sailed the high seas in a hijacked ship he called *Queen Anne's Revenge*, journeying with forty cannons and a crew of 300 pirates [3].

In command of his fellow pirates, Blackbeard attacked merchant ships filled with valuables, stealing food, weapons, and liquor

[1]. He exerted complete control over his crew by simply firing the gun he always kept on him. If he didn't release an occasional bullet into one or two of his crewmen, they might've forgotten who was in charge [1].

Stricken with syphilis, Blackbeard even ordered the strategic looting of medicine. In 1718, he held a prominent Charleston citizen hostage while negotiating the gentleman's ransom [1]. The famously late delivery of the medicine led to the begrudging release of his prisoners, who were left shaken and humiliatingly unclothed [1].

Wherever Blackbeard was originally from, he favored sailing the Caribbean and the eastern coast of America, antagonizing ships about to enter or leave harbor [3]. The crews of the merchant ships he targeted suffered torture, and loads of cargo were stolen without remorse. Despite enjoying protection under his fearsome reputation, Blackbeard wasn't known to have actually killed anyone [1].

But his greatest public relations weapon was his lengthy, haggardly black beard. Blackbeard intentionally grew his facial hair to impressive lengths, some saying his beard reached the waistline of his six-foot-four frame. Thick and knotty, his dark beard was wild enough for matches to be woven into it and lit whenever he ventured out to battle [1]. As Blackbeard fought to snatch the riches aboard merchant ships, wafts of smoke rose from his beard and encircled his menacing face. His devilish image struck paralyzing fear into the hearts of his enemies. And so, Blackbeard carefully solidified his enduring legacy as a savage pirate whose very name struck fear into those of high and low status alike.

Managing the care of such an enormous beard must not have been easy for an eighteenth-century pirate constantly at sea. Proper hygiene was an endless struggle aboard ships that spent months teetering on ocean waves. Dirty conditions afflicted most pirates with lice and fleas [4]. Leaping over the ship's railing to wash their hair in the salty ocean water wasn't appealing, as leaving the ship to be potentially carried by currents was a dangerous choice [4]. Plus, in the superstitious minds of pirates, sea monsters lurked everywhere in the terrible seas.

Pirates who intended to stay as clean and hygienic as possible shaved with iron blades, or the occasional shard of glass. But not Blackbeard. Trusting a shipmate to shave a fellow crew member was riddled with dangers. A buoyant pirate ship frequently heaved on the boisterous waves, making it likely that the slightest misstep during a shave would result in a painful laceration, with the very real possibility of a horrible ensuing infection and a long, drawn-out death. Naturally, in an effort to avoid the agony, plus the desire to instill fear upon his enemies, Blackbeard decided to forego the daily burden of shaving and grow his beard to disproportionate lengths.

Of course, a thick, ungroomed beard full of pests invited its own pain and discomfort. It's almost unquestionable that his irascible temper was heightened by the constant, itchy pain from the bites of pests concealed in his facial hair. Perhaps his fiery personality, amplified by his ongoing physical discomfort, compelled Blackbeard to carry out ever more merciless attacks on the merchant ships that dared cross his path. Needless to say, the lack of hygiene aboard ships, the ongoing battles, and the prevalence of diseases, like scurvy and syphilis, ensured pirating was never intended to be a long-lived career.

A pirate who'd just entered the illicit profession could expect to live a maximum of five years. Such was the fate of Blackbeard. He perished in a calculated ambush, suffering five gunshot wounds and twenty-five cuts of the sword, before his decapitated head was victoriously hung from the ship's bowsprit [1].

Now, had Blackbeard only had access to a modern convenience—the electric shaver—he'd have avoided such a frightening fate. Shaving each morning with his handheld device, he'd have prevented his beard from growing awfully long and untamable. Without his beard, Blackbeard would've struggled to establish his fearsome persona—and would've ultimately failed as a pirate. Clean-shaven, the unsuccessful, unintimidating Blackbeard could've resumed his work as a privateer, the legal form of pirating. The electric shaver, in short, would've saved his life and allowed him to live beyond his thirty-eight years.

Of course, without his beard and his frightening exploits across the Caribbean Sea, Blackbeard wouldn't have risen to his legendary heights. At least, though, he'd have lived longer than his five years as a feared pirate. But electric shavers were only invented by Colonel Jacob Schick in 1930—over 200 years after the era of rampant seafaring pirates.

Blackbeard would've enjoyed a close-cut, clean shave with his wet-dry-electric shaver. Cleaning the shaver would've been a breeze with the included cleaning pod. The pirate could've put all his energy into looting, rather than catching random facial hairs. A smooth, effortless shave awaited Blackbeard, had only the electric shaver been around during the Golden Age of Piracy. Alas, it wasn't, and so we are left with stories about the grand exploits of the infamous Blackbeard, a pirate who'd plundered enough riches to purchase a golden chest of the highest-quality electric razors available today.

20

MONA LISA AND PHOTO METADATA

Camera-friendly people have existed since the dawn of human-kind. What did photogenic people do before the invention of the digital camera? These alluring folks sat for extraordinary paint-ers, like Leonardo DaVinci. One such photogenic woman was Mona Lisa. Leonard DaVinci painted her exquisite portrait sometime be-tween 1503 and 1519. Simple and unadorned, Mona Lisa didn't need the help of shimmering diamonds or the trappings of a flamboyant costume to hold the public's fancy for over 500 hundred years.

Rather, all she did was pose for Leonardo DaVinci, wearing a dark robe, a sheer veil, and an enigmatic smile that captured the imagination of people worldwide [1]. DaVinci worked patiently to achieve a realism unprecedented at the time of his contemporar-ies, including Michelangelo and Raphael. He studied earnestly to gain a profound understanding of how the human skeleton took shape beneath the skin and rendered his portrait with the skill of an enlightened Renaissance painter [1]. He expertly played with light and shadow, as evidenced by Mona Lisa's softly sculpted face [1]. The accomplished artist also delicately rendered her translu-cent veil and dark tresses on the poplar wood panel [1].

DaVinci's masterpiece in oil earned praise and recognition even as he started to paint it in 1503 and intermittently added layers here and there over the years [2]. His contemporaries marveled at the artist's congruency between humanity and nature, which he presented with harmonious style [2]. DaVinci's Mona Lisa became the epitome of artistic skill for future portrait painters [2].

While it's clear that DaVinci completed a remarkable painting, what was not so apparent was the identity of the sitter. An alternate title of the work was *La Giocanda*. DaVinci's biographer speculated that the sitter was Lisa del Giocondo, the spouse of the Florentine merchant, Francesco di Bartolemeo del Giocondo [2]. But no one had stumbled upon records showing he commissioned the work [2]. A second far-fetched but plausible speculation was that the sitter was modeled after DaVinci himself, considering the facial features were peculiarly similar [2]. To this day, no one can confirm the identity of Mona Lisa.

Mona Lisa has enchanted people all over the world, not only because of the masterful quality of the work, but because the oil painting was housed at the Louvre—the French museum with the greatest number of visitors in the world [1]. Historically, the painting had remained a valuable piece in the royal art collection of Francis I, the king of France [1]. Later, Napoleon Bonaparte hung the Mona Lisa on the walls of his lavish Tuileries bedroom for a brief stint, until it finally arrived at its final home in the impressive Louvre Museum in 1804 [1].

Increasing the popularity of the Mona Lisa was the fact that no one could pinpoint the identity of the woman with the peaceful gaze and demure half-smile. Even art thieves couldn't resist her elusive seduction and stole the painting from the Louvre in 1911 [2]. The media frenzy surrounding the theft immediately catapulted the Mona Lisa to international celebrity status [2]. The heist was comical in nature and infused the whole shebang with a colorful story: the rogue who stole the work of art had trouble selling it because of the media frenzy and resorted to tucking it away in the false bottom of a dusty old trunk [2]. The painting was eventually found and returned to hang in the Louvre. By then, the French had realized what a treasure the illustrious painting was and celebrated its return [2]. Still, after all the fuss, the real Mona Lisa remained an unsolvable mystery.

Leonardo DaVinci could've satisfied the worldwide curiosity surrounding the Mona Lisa had he only had access to a digital camera and the modern convenience associated with it—photo metadata. The nearly eight million annual visitors to the Louvre would have looked upon the mild-mannered lady in the sublime portrait not with endless questions, but with satisfactory answers. DaVinci could've utilized his natural genius to skillfully operate a digital camera during the sixteenth century and taken a breathtaking photograph that would be remembered to this day. He was a polymath, after all, knowledgeable about a wide range of topics, from science and engineering to art; it wouldn't have been a stretch for him to excel in photography as much as he did in painting. As was customary for artists, DaVinci would have instructed Mona Lisa to pose for the shot. She'd have eagerly followed his direction to help create the loveliest possible image of her—a portrait photo that would've endured as long as DaVinci's painting.

But what would've gratified awe-struck onlookers was the invaluable metadata. DaVinci would've recorded all the details necessary to identify the subject in his professional photo. As photographer—in lieu of painter—DaVinci would have noted in the metadata file when the photo was taken, where it was shot, and how it was created. These descriptive details would've been clearly visible on the digital camera's screen. Most importantly, the metadata would have described the content of the photo—specifically, the name of the subject.

DaVinci's metadata would've eliminated all the guesswork for admirers of the Mona Lisa. We'd know whether she was truly Lisa del Giocondo, a female version of DaVinci, or someone else entirely. Freud wouldn't have had the opportunity to suggest that Mona Lisa was DaVinci's mother, because we'd have known for sure by perusing the metadata that she wasn't painted from the artist's memory of her.

Plus, admirers of the Mona Lisa would've known the exact date DaVinci's photographic portrait was taken. Art historians theorize that DaVinci painted his world-famous work sporadically within a span of sixteen years in Florence, but no one can determine the date of completion. Instead, had Davinci taken a professional headshot of Mona Lisa and entered the metadata as a responsible photographer would, art lovers would've felt the gratification of knowing precisely when the work was finished.

But photo metadata didn't see the light of day until digital cameras were invented in 1975—nearly 500 years after DaVinci started working on the most famous painting in the world. Every person of culture recognizes Mona Lisa, but none can say with certainty her true name.

Nowadays, whenever a three-quarter headshot is taken with a slight turn sideways, onlookers can immediately identify the individual by reviewing the photo metadata. Long gone are the days when no one could accurately determine who was the primary subject of a fabulous work of art. A modern convenience, photo metadata leaves no one guessing. But Mona Lisa still does.

21

CHICHEN ITZA'S MAYAN PRIESTS AND ESCALATORS

Chichen Itza in Mexico's Yucatan Peninsula was home to one of the Americas' greatest pyramids, El Castillo. The awed Spanish conquistadors who set sights on this colossal stone structure centuries ago gave it the famous moniker, which translated to the Castle.

Wiping the sweat from their brows, the laboring Mayan classes built the pyramid around 1100 C.E. [1]. These precocious builders did not use metal tools. Instead, the Mayans worked with stone tools and those made from wood or animal bone to erect entire cities, complete with intersecting roads, as well as the city's pinnacle structure—the Castle pyramid, the cherished religious center for the civilization [2].

Constructing the pyramid required the Mayan architects to rely heavily on their highly sophisticated system of mathematics [2]. Designing the pyramid required advanced skills in algebra, geometry, and trigonometry. Bringing the project to fruition further required calculating the number of potential structural issues. With their success in fulfilling their vision for a wondrous pyramid built with a temple at the top, the ancient Mayans unquestionably proved their ingenuity.

Built with four equal sets of stairs on each side, the Castle pyramid was a marvelous feat of engineering. Master builders performed careful calculations to construct exactly ninety-one steps on each of the pyramid's four sides [3]. Combining the number of steps on each staircase, plus the temple at the summit, totaled 365—the number of days in the Mayan solar year [3].

Reaching the temple positioned at the tip-top of the Castle pyramid required ascending the ninety-one steps from any one side. The Herculean task of climbing this intimidating number of steps was reserved for none other than the esteemed Mayan priests. These powerful men of faith performed rituals at the top of the pyramid, where they'd be as close as humanly possible to the gods in the starry heavens [3].

While the top of the Castle pyramid held celestial wonders, the bottom was believed to be a place of dreadful fright. Rivers and underground caves wove an intricate maze under the limestone bedrock [3]. Fresh water was drawn from these cavities underneath the Castle [3]. But the water systems held a more sinister significance: the entrances to these underground formations were thought to be doorways to a fiery hell. The Castle was the center of the Mayan world, quite possibly the midpoint between the upper realms of a glorious heaven and the depths of doom in a terrifying underworld [3]. And it was up to the religious whims of the Mayan priests to ascend or descend the staircase.

Mayan priests held powerful roles in the ancient world. It was their job to keep the uncongenial demons in the underworld from engaging in mischief in the inhabited earthly realm [2]. The priests performed ceremonies, offering precious minerals and stones, like gold and jade, plus the occasional human [3].

The power held by the ancient Mayan priesthood was just a wee step under that of Mayan nobility. The priests' influence spread far and wide in the lives of ordinary and extraordinary Mayan people. Priests served not only as religious figures, but as teachers, astronomers, and healers [4]. Administering the city was a primary task too [4]. These highly regarded religious individuals advised the Mayan ruling elite about civil affairs and dealings with neighboring cities [4]. Priests performed divination and interpreted omens. Marriages didn't take place unless the priest gave his wholehearted approval. After all, it was the priest who could discern the realistic prospects of a marital union better than the romantic partners.

Clearly, given such absolute power and influence over the Mayan people, the least ethical of priests could have profited personally by taking advantage of their innocent awe [5]. While it was unclear as to what extent priests may have abused their divine privileges, one thing was certain: summiting the ninety-one steps to the temple required incredible physical endurance.

Religious ceremonies were common in ancient Mayan culture. The God of Rain, the God of Sun, and the God of Maize had to be appeased daily [2]. The Mayan priests showed remarkable physical fitness in traversing the lengthy stone staircase up and down each day to access the temple and perform the requisite ceremonies. While such physical feats were practical for priests boasting ruddy youth, the aged ones experienced far greater challenges. It was no wonder that the young sons of older priests succeeded them when the ascensions to the summit got tough.

What these aged Mayan priests needed to get them up and down from the strategically positioned temple was an invaluable modern convenience—the escalator. Had this adaptable contraption been around at the time of ancient Mayans, their priests would have enjoyed far lengthier careers. Simply, they'd have been able to ascend and descend the staircase well into old age. Rather than hike up the ninety-one stone steps, all they needed to do was hop onto the escalator, hold onto the railing without being irked by it moving faster than the stairs, then hop off at the top. A few steps into the interior of the temple would've ensured they were as close to the heavens as possible.

And the escalator would have been equally convenient for ascending the upper realm as well as entering the mouth of the underworld—whichever option fancied the priest. After all, the escalator has the ability to transport individuals upward or downward. If need be, the Castle could've been built with two downward-moving escalators and two upward-moving escalators—easing the leg pain the priests undeniably felt upon climbing the long sets of stairs.

Instead of the Mayan priests summoning immense patience to diligently climb all ninety-one steps, an escalator would've effortlessly transported them in fluid motion. No longer would the one-dimensional staircase have tired them out long before retirement age. Rather, with the revolving steps of the escalator, even reaching the sky would've had no limits.

But the modern escalator was only invented in the twentieth century by George Wheeler [6]. Several similar inventions had been patented since 1859, but Wheeler's was the one that took off. In 1909, for instance, a demonstration of an early mechanical escalator at Coney Island took people up leisurely, but these men in proper suits and hats had to slide back down on a mat—utterly absurd for a well-dressed gentleman [6]. Naturally, this particular version of the escalator failed to seize the public's imagination. And it would've been just as unbecoming for a respectable ancient Mayan priest to slide downward on a plain mat from the temple above.

George Wheeler's version of the escalator stuck, however. Steps appeared on the floor and flattened once they reached the destination floor [6]. The concept of a moving staircase burst into the spotlight at the Paris Exposition in 1900, winning an award for functional design [6]. Bloomingdale's and Macy's replaced their staircases with escalators [6]. Train stations followed soon after [6]. Workplaces installed escalators in their office buildings to enhance efficiency [6]. Employees no longer had to cut twenty irreplaceable minutes off their lunch hour to trudge up and down flights of stairs.

Escalators equaled the playing field for shoppers and office employees [6]. People of any fitness level could reach upper floors without succumbing to complete physical exhaustion. This modern convenience erased the possibility that shoppers would lose interest in purchasing items just because they hung on a rack on the uppermost floors. Likewise, with the help of escalators built into the four sides of the Castle, the ancient Mayan priests would've sustained genuine zeal in their lifelong careers, instead of passing on the torch to their young sons once their tired quadriceps hopelessly gave out on them.

22

CHRISTOPHER COLUMBUS AND
OVER-THE-HORIZON RADAR

While Christopher Columbus was no scholar, he was a self-educated young man. He scoured the chapters in ancient books, from the travelogue *The Travels of Marco Polo* to Pliny's *Natural History*, to formulate his unique theories of the world [1]. His intensive studies led him to believe that the enormous wealth and exotic spices of India, Japan, and China could be had by sailing west instead of east.

In fact, Columbus convinced himself that sailing westward was the shortest route from Europe to Asia [1]. As a master navigator, he intended to prove his theory to the world. In the process, he planned to bring back to Spain the gold, silver, pearls, spices, and silks that he believed awaited him in Asia.

Columbus was no stranger to oceanic adventures. At the age of twenty-six, he made voyages to Iceland and Ireland [2]. Five to eight years later, between 1482 and 1485, he sailed to the Portuguese fortress São Jorge da Mina [2]. He gained invaluable knowledge about navigation and wind systems, which would prove critical during his future voyages to the west [2].

In 1484, Columbus made the bold decision to cross the Atlantic. His requests for financial assistance were denied by King John II of Portugal. It wasn't until 1492 that he finally received royal support from King Ferdinand and Queen Isabella, both of whom entertained notions of enhancing the crown's wealth and status by financing a transatlantic voyage that promised immense riches.

On August 3, 1492, a fleet of three maiden ships, the Niña, the Pinta, and the Santa María, set sail on a westerly course with about ninety treasure-seeking sailors. After an uneventful month at sea, the crew noticed signs of land: vegetation floating on the waves and birds squawking in the sky. But October soon came, and land was nowhere to be seen. Columbus' men grew agitated, complaining with inconsolable angst that they wouldn't have enough supplies to return home [2].

As a defiant Columbus sailed onward on the Niña and braved the tumultuous waves of the Atlantic, his sailors on the Pinta finally sighted land [2]. It was October 12, and Columbus stopped briefly to plant the royal flag on the islands of the Bahamas [2]. Two weeks later, he landed in Cuba, erroneously believing he'd found Japan [2]. The master navigator was a mess of confusion at sea. Still seeking the shores of China, he ended up in Haiti on December 6, calling the island Hispaniola [2].

Columbus knew the world was as round as a Rio Red grapefruit. Naturally, he believed he could reach the Far East by sailing directly westward instead of eastward around the coast of the African continent, as his contemporaries had done [3]. He felt confident in his plan, but neglected to imagine the possibility that gigantic landmasses would be in his way.

If only Columbus' small ships were fitted with a modern convenience—the over-the-horizon radar—he'd have known during his voyage that a large continent lay between Spain and his intended destination. North America would have been immediately detected by the frequency of radio waves emanating from the radar. However, no ordinary radar would do, since the most basic of gadgets would've been unable to see over the curve of the earth's surface. But an over-the-horizon radar, built specifically to see beyond this limitation, would've suited the exploration needs of Columbus just fine.

The long-range detection capabilities of the over-the-horizon radar would've found all sorts of signs of land nearby. The sailors aboard the Niña, Pinta, and Santa María would've been surprised yet relieved to see the blue and green shadings on the radar's screen, indicating the presence of flocks of sandhill cranes [4]. Swarms of grasshoppers and beetles, too, would've shown up on the radar as splotches of yellow and green [4]. Equally riveting to Columbus' sailors would've been the smoke from California wildfires that would've appeared on the radar as blue and green hues [4].

Most importantly, the over-the-horizon radar onboard Columbus' ships would've detected land from a range of 2,000 nautical miles. Columbus would've observed this presence of land precisely at the halfway point between Spain and North America. The distance between Europe and the coast of the Americas was approximately 4,700 miles, making land observable on the radar at slightly over 2,000 miles. That meant Columbus and his men would've confirmed the presence of land in September rather than October—an entire month earlier. And his sailors wouldn't have felt the need to gripe about the lack of provisions for their return journey, but rather leapt for joy at the prospects of finding treasures of gold, silks, and spices.

Over-the-horizon radars, however, didn't come into existence until the mid-1970's—almost 500 years after Columbus' voyage to the Americas. Although Columbus never set foot on North American soil, the United States adopted the use of over-the-horizon radars, along with Russia, China, and Australia.

If only over-the-horizon radars had been available in the fifteenth century and Columbus smartly installed them on his three ships, he'd have known that he was about to sail into the shallow shores of a massive land mass that rivaled the size of mainland China. In all truth, he might've legitimately confused China with the United States, since both were similar in their total surface area, at 3.6 million square miles. But with China being 2.2 percent bigger than the United States, the experienced navigator would've at least stopped to ponder the reason for the size difference. Perhaps it wasn't China, after all? This lightbulb moment might've changed the course of European exploration.

In the end, Columbus believed he'd found a new route to the East Indies. But he didn't, and the over-the-horizon radar, had his ships been equipped with the device, would've clearly illustrated this. Since Columbus failed to discover the limitless stores of silks, pearls, and spices on his voyages westward, it should've been a clear indication that something was amiss during his travels. Nevertheless, a modern convenience, like over-the-horizon radar, would've been a fifteenth-century explorer's dream.

23

BEN FRANKLIN AND SMART EYEGLASSES

One of America's esteemed Founding Fathers, Benjamin Franklin was credited with several notable inventions, including bifocals. While he devised the "double spectacles," the use of eyeglasses for improving myopia was first recorded in the late thirteenth century in northern Italy [1, 3]. Also, in thirteenth-century Europe, lenses were used to correct age-related presbyopia. Humans suffered nearsightedness long before then, which explained the discovery of optical-wear remnants from 1000 B.C.E [2].

Nearsightedness wasn't always the epidemic it is today. Vision problems have existed since the time of early primates, but our human ancestors rarely needed the help of eyeglasses to see details up close [3]. Early humans spent most of their time outdoors hunting, gathering, weaving, farming, and cooking. Without having to regularly resort to weather almanacs, hunting manuals, reference books listing edible berries, and cookbooks, their eyesight hardly suffered.

Regular reading caused the eyes to focus on up-close text. Eyes grew longer to facilitate this close work, worsening long-distance vision [3]. For much of the early human timeline, reading wasn't a daily occurrence. The only materials read by humans were the clay tablet, papyrus scroll, and much later, paper documents, and the occasional book. Since our early predecessors didn't prioritize reading in their daily lives, nearsightedness never had the chance to balloon into a major problem.

Only during the Renaissance, when reading began to represent the sophisticated thinking of the intellectual and elite classes, did eyeglasses start becoming increasingly necessary. In the thirteenth century, Europe was a hub for glassmaking. Tucked into bulging bags of tradable goods, newly invented spectacles were carried by merchants across the world to places as far east as Asia [3].

Four centuries later, in 1706, Benjamin Franklin was born in Boston, Massachusetts. As a boy, Franklin learned to read early. He was an avid bookworm, perusing books at every opportunity while also teaching himself to write. Poetry grew to be his first love [5]. But after failing in his multiple attempts to compose works of poetic grace, he judiciously switched to writing prose—and what a wise choice it was. He admitted that writing persuasive and witty prose was a key factor in his professional success [5].

At the age of sixteen, Franklin wrote and published in his brother's newspaper, the *New-England Courant*, a series of moral essays under the feminine pseudonym Silence Dogood [5]. No one speculated that the author wasn't a matronly widow with enough life experience to showcase exuberant wit. Ten years later, Franklin wrote and published his *Poor Richard's Almanac* under another pseudonym, Richard Saunders [6]. The almanac was a sensation, and Franklin continued writing and publishing them annually for the next twenty-six years [6]. He concluded the series by writing a preface known today as *The Way to Wealth*, which was published in the almanac's final edition in 1758 [5].

Knowledgeable on a wide range of worldly topics, from social policies to scientific mysteries, Franklin continued disseminating his storehouse of knowledge through newspapers, like the *Pennsylvania Gazette*. He penned his autobiography much later in life, a time when he also helped draft the Declaration of Independence.

During these last stages of his lengthy literary career, he discovered his need to see without the burden of having to alternate eyeglasses. No longer a youth boasting ruddy health, Franklin had aged. He'd developed both nearsightedness and farsightedness, a problem without a single solution to correct the two vision conditions. The common remedy in the eighteenth century was to repeatedly switch eyeglasses. A pair of nearsighted glasses would sit at the tip of Franklin's nose as he read the morning newspaper. He'd pluck his distance glasses resting atop his head whenever a gentleman popped in and Franklin needed to clearly see whose friendly face was at the door. Constantly fumbling with two pairs of eyeglasses frustrated wearers who required both to function in daily life. Franklin wasn't immune, either, and was determined to resolve his irritations surrounding the repeated swapping of eyeglasses.

Franklin, a tinkerer by nature and circumstance, was no stranger to bringing useful inventions to vivid life. He'd invented the lightning rod after flying a kite in a rainstorm, the Franklin Stove upon feeling a shiver in the midst of the chilly east coast winters, swim fins at age eleven, the urinary catheter to help his brother stricken with a kidney stone, the glorious-sounding glass armonica—and bifocals [1].

Motivated by annoyance, Franklin commissioned one half of each lens of his distance and reading glasses to be sliced horizontally, then reassembled as one pair [1]. The lens for seeing distant objects took up the upper half, and the lens for reading sat on the bottom half [1]. Wearing his new bifocals, Franklin no longer felt forced to awkwardly search his pockets or the top of his head for the right pair of eyeglasses to support the specified task at hand. He could simply wear one pair of eyeglasses throughout the day and see as clearly as he had as a boy with twenty-twenty vision.

Had a modern convenience—smart eyeglasses—been around in the eighteenth century, when Franklin experienced his vision dilemmas, he'd have been tickled pink to own a pair. Available with prescription lenses, smart eyeglasses would've given Franklin not only the ability to scan the written word, but augment reality. And what forward-thinking eighteenth-century American wouldn't have wanted to experience such a once-in-a-lifetime novelty?

Franklin kept himself busy, traveling between America and England during his adult life. By sporting a pair of smart eyeglasses featuring a reliable navigation system, Franklin would've been able to find his way around London's intricate maze of streets [7]. With a population of three-quarters of a million people in the eighteenth century, London was noisy and overcrowded. Asking for directions would've gotten Franklin lost more frequently than he'd have liked. But with the help of the reliable navigation system built into his trusty pair of smart eyeglasses, Franklin would've quickly located the many London theaters he enjoyed frequenting in his youthful, indulgent heyday.

With hands-free access to the internet, Franklin, wearing his modest pair of smart eyeglasses, would've looked up online answers to questions about morals, natural philosophy, or politics— knowledgeably arguing his points with members of his Leather Apron Club. Conducting political affairs would've been similarly facilitated. Franklin would've chatted via text with the rest of the Founding Fathers about making specific adjustments to the Declaration of Independence, scheduled political meetings with Thomas Jefferson, and given speeches with the smart eyeglasses' teleprompter-like capabilities.

More than anything else, Franklin would've enhanced the functionality of smart eyeglasses at his whim, and with much fanfare. Applying his signature inventiveness, he'd have viewed smart eyeglasses with ingenious insight, elevating the gadget to new technological heights that today's societies couldn't possibly fathom. After all, no other eighteenth century innovator came up with the brilliant concepts of the lightning rod, or bifocals.

But smart eyeglasses launched only as recently as the twenty-first century, 300 years after the productive era of Benjamin

Franklin. Regardless of the unfortunate timing, one thing is as clear as twenty-twenty vision: had smart eyeglasses been available at the time of Franklin, he'd have taken this modern convenience to unprecedented levels and given himself, his contemporaries, and later generations, a new vision for the limitless potentials of future technology.

24

INUIT IGLOOS AND REVERSIBLE CEILING FANS

In 1050 C.E., Inuit frequently traveled on hunting expeditions amid fierce Arctic Canadian winters. Their sole means of lodging against the howling wind and biting cold was the igloo, a temporary form of housing built to shelter Inuit hunters for the extended duration of the hunt. Assembled with blocks of dry, carefully chosen snowdrift and cut with knives made from whale bone, these nine-foot by twelve-foot accommodations housed all members of one Inuit family [1].

Relaxing on several caribou furs laid out over blocks of snow, Inuit socialized around the oil lamp consisting of a base of polished soapstone, oil from animal blubber, and a wick of woven cotton-grass [2]. The smokeless flame, combined with the body heat of several Inuit, raised the temperature inside the igloo to a balmy thirty degrees Fahrenheit, toasty compared to the minus forty degrees Fahrenheit of whipping cold outside [3]. A hole cut in the center at the top of the igloo allowed heat to escape.

Inuit fished upon breaking the sea ice a short distance from their igloo, strategically built as close to the sea as possible. The catch was quickly cooked over the oil lamp inside the igloo and relished by the entire family of man, woman, and child. Salmon was ravenously consumed dried or smoked [4]. Whitefish could be sliced thin, then eaten raw [4]. Hunters harpooned seals as they navigated one-person kayaks on the open sea. Seal oil was a useful fuel for cooking, while simultaneously serving as a delicious dipping sauce to enhance food flavors [4]. Moose that unwittingly wandered into the hunters' line of sight were killed and devoured [4]. Likewise, ptarmigan and geese were hunted and served on plates made of bone [4].

The Canadian Inuit chatted in Inuktitut dialects, like Inuvialuktun or Inuinnaqtun, savoring the food and convivial social atmosphere inside the warm igloo—which never melted, so long as the temperature outside remained below freezing [5]. The preservation of the igloo required a harmonious balance between the warmth inside— created by the oil lamp plus body heat—and the bitter Arctic Canadian air outside. Naturally, the heat source inside the igloo melted the packed snow blocks slightly, but the frigid air outside refroze the snowmelt, adding a second icy but solid layer of protective insulation [6].

Clearly, the atmosphere inside the igloo was cozy, even as Arctic blizzards chaotically hurled snow and wind. It certainly helped that Inuit genes predisposed them to an increased toleration of cold. The problem with heating an igloo, however, occurred when the cooler air traveled to the bottom of the igloo, forcing the upper section to remain warm. Warm air has the natural tendency to rise, wasting all the valuable warmth in the upper areas of even a well-built igloo.

Anyone who lived in an igloo, even temporarily, knew that the shelter's livable bottom was where maximum warmth was essential. Warmth at the dome of a single-family igloo was hardly necessary, as no one inhabited that space. At five-foot-four, the average Inuit would've found it impossible to enjoy the warmth at the top of the dome, even while standing upright inside the twelve-foot-high igloo. The exception was when an igloo was built with tiers, but these were intended to house twenty people.

Now, had a modern convenience—the reversible ceiling fan—been available to early Inuit hunters of Arctic Canada, their living quarters inside the igloo would have seen dramatic improvement. The blades of the reversible ceiling fan would've spun clockwise to create a gentle updraft, pushing the warm air hovering wastefully at the dome of the igloo downward toward the living space, where it would've warmed the whole family. Building terraces (reserved for larger igloos) for individuals to sleep at an elevated height would have exposed them to the cold from the hole at the top of the snow structure. This modern convenience was just what an Inuit family needed to double the warmth inside their domed quarters during the chilly winter hunting season. However, ceiling fans didn't see the light of day until 1882, when they were invented by Philip Diehl, Thomas Edison's forward-thinking contemporary.

Unfortunately, though ceiling fans are commonplace in households today, many homeowners remain unaware of the fact that they could be reversed to improve heat distribution and save on energy costs in winter. Had reversible ceiling fans only been around in the eleventh century, the Inuit would have enjoyed pleasantly warmer indoor temperatures during the winter hunting season and sheltered far more comfortably.

Furthermore, investing in a light fixture would've made the fan a superb multi-functional device, as artificial light would've shone during the dark Arctic Canadian winter months. A remote would have splendidly tripled the convenience, controlling the direction of the reversible ceiling fan from a distance. In blistery winter conditions, the reversible ceiling fan outweighed any modern convenience designed to circulate warm air—whether that be inside an Inuit hunter's igloo, or today's single-family home.

25

GENGHIS KHAN AND THE PATERNITY TEST

The earth shook when Genghis Khan was thrust into Mongolia near Lake Baikal in 1162 C.E. Living a childhood of obscurity, the Mongol steadily raised his insignificant status to impressive heights. It wasn't long before this warrior-ruler created the largest land empire ever known, surpassing the brilliant military achievements of his predecessors, Alexander the Great and Julius Caesar.

The Mongol wasn't born as the mighty Genghis Khan, which translates into "Universal Ruler," but as the humble Temujin [1]. He earned his famed moniker by exerting his inborn fighting prowess, which won him huge portions of central Asia and China. The warrior's nonstop imperial expansion continued west to Syria, Korea, and Poland. At his empire's height, Genghis Khan controlled over eleven million contiguous square miles of territory, stretching from the coast of Japan to the Carpathian Mountain ranges of Eastern Europe [2]. Upon uniting his nation, he was proclaimed Chinggis Khan—but to the west, he was familiarly known as Genghis Khan.

Genghis Khan's achievements endured. He advanced literacy by adopting the Uyghur script, which served as the basis for the Uyghur-Mongolian writing system [3]. He was one of the first rulers to encourage freedom of religion [3]. Under the social policies of Genghis Khan, women were no longer shockingly sold, and foreign ambassadors were shielded by diplomatic immunity [3].

The emperor left a far more lasting legacy, however, one that continues to the present day. During Genghis Khan's numerous bold conquests, the most beautiful women captured were specially reserved to satisfy his voracious, lustful appetite. This highly fertile warrior was estimated to have fathered hundreds, and some say thousands, of children.

Daughters of Genghis Khan held important roles that influenced his diplomacies and strategies for warfare. These women married leaders of nations surrounding Mongolia, a tactic that solidified alliances indefinitely [4]. The famed Silk Road was controlled by none other than Genghis Khan's powerful daughters [4]. Experienced in warfare, they fought skillfully alongside their father's male soldiers during campaigns in Persia, China, and other foreign nations marked for conquest [4].

During Genghis Khan's rule, his children profited from his material riches, wielded immense power, and played influential roles in his wars. And these were only the children Genghis Khan knew about. Given his tendency to claim women during conquests near and far, the warrior was likely to have sired a greater number of children he'd never met, children who never grew up to hold roles of power, or revel in their father's lavish imperial wealth.

Doubling the misfortune was that the women who bore Genghis Khan's children may have had little support in raising his legions of progeny. Family setbacks, expected challenges, and societal disapproval would have left devastating wounds on these women. These females should've had the means to prove that Genghis Khan was their children's father and fight for their just rewards, from riches to status.

The paternity test, however, would have achieved exactly that, giving these women the much-needed support to raise their boys and girls securely and comfortably. In fact, once grown, these unknown children of Genghis Khan would have held prestigious military roles in his wars or been strategically married off to wealthy leaders of neighboring clans. Since they'd have been instant contenders for the bounties of his wars, their lives would have been as glorious as his recognized children.

But the DNA test used to confirm paternity was only invented by British geneticist Sir Alex Jeffreys in 1984—over 800 years after Genghis Khan's series of raids outside of Mongolia. The DNA test affirmed biological relationships between humans. All that was needed was a cheek swab to lift a sample for testing. Within a day, results would've shown whether Genghis Khan's DNA and the mother's DNA matched the child's, thereby proving this genius warrior was indeed the biological father of a little girl or boy.

Surprisingly—or perhaps unsurprisingly, due to his prolific reproductive capabilities—Genghis Khan's 800-year-old Mongol lineage continues to this day. Geneticists discovered that one in every 200 men currently alive in central Asia are relatives of Genghis Khan [5]. These sixteen million-plus men share nearly identical Y-chromosome sequences with the Mongol ruler [5]. Genghis Khan clearly had a lot of sons, who in turn fathered a lot of boys [6].

The ultimate proof of Genghis Khan's enduring lineage would've been a DNA test. But accurate results would've required extracting a sample from the remains of this great warrior-ruler. Unfortunately for science, his tomb was never found. Regardless, had this modern convenience been available to each of the countless women with whom Genghis Khan fervently mated, their children would've rightly received exalted privileges. And to this day, a huge chunk of society would've enjoyed a massive confidence boost, knowing Genghis Khan loomed high in their family tree. These men would've naturally strived to emulate their distinguished ancestor, taking calculated risks, living with less fear, and generally moving outside their comfort zone to accomplish bigger and better things. Such personal enhancements would've been the indirect result of one modern convenience: the life-changing paternity test.

26

WILLIAM TELL AND THE MODERN CROSSBOW

William Tell symbolized the bravery and indomitable spirit of Switzerland. Like the noble King Arthur of Wales, the story of William Tell was steeped in legend. Tell might've been a real historical figure, or his admirable feats may have been a conglomeration of the notable deeds of others. For the sake of lore, Tell was a hero during the fourteenth century when Austria imposed harsh rule over the Swiss people, its regime led by the tyrannical agent of the Hapsburg duke of Austria, Bailiff Gessler [1].

In a display of oppression, Gessler hung a hat on a pole in the middle of the town's busy public square. The Austrian trumpets blared, and after they halted their cacophony of subjugation, Gessler demanded to everyone within earshot that they respectfully remove their hat upon passing and bow [1, 2].

A proud and dignified Swiss, Tell felt the need to rebel against Gessler's humiliating request. He confidently strutted past the hat, drooping like a limp fish on the pole, and refused to uncover his head. Gessler's men witnessed Tell's bold act of defiance and dragged him before the angry Gessler [2]. Tell couldn't bring himself to bow down to Gessler either, much less his floppy hat.

As a tyrant, Gessler's rage was legitimate. If one Swiss man had the audacity to defy him, other residents wouldn't hesitate to do the same [2]. The bailiff feared a rebellion, and decided to make an example of Tell. Receiving respect was Gessler's intent, and he'd force it by inflicting a cruel form of punishment.

Tell was an accomplished hunter, highly skilled in using the crossbow. No one living in the picturesque mountains of the Swiss Alps could shoot an arrow with Tell's speed and precision. Gessler became aware of Tell's extraordinary talent and used it to improvise his penalty. The bailiff bellowed gruffly to the hunter that he demonstrate the extent of his expertise [2]. And to achieve that end, Gessler forced Tell to shoot an apple off the top of his son's head from 120 paces away in the middle of the crowded public square [1, 2]. If he failed, both Tell and his boy would be executed.

As a father with immense love for his young son, Tell was overwhelmed with nervous angst. Sweat dripped from his brow, and he wrung his damp hands. The famed hunter beseeched Gessler, asking what would happen if his son moved or his hand trembled upon releasing the arrow [2]. Indifferent to the desperate pleas of the loving father, the grim Gessler insisted he shoot.

Mustering all his courage, Tell clutched his crossbow, fitted the arrow, and took careful aim. His brave son, believing wholeheartedly in his father, stood in the public square without flinching [2]. The spectators surrounding the square gasped, letting not one word escape their gaping mouths. Tell's arrow sped through the cool Swiss air, like a knife sliced through soft butter, and struck the center of the apple. The fruit fell, as did a second arrow from under Tell's coat.

Gessler, upon seeing the spare arrow fall, demanded to know its purpose [2]. Defiant as ever, Tell roared that his second arrow was for the center of the bailiff's cold heart, if his first arrow had harmed his son [2]. "And with this second arrow," Tell declared, "I surely wouldn't have missed."

Tell had proved to Gessler and the Swiss people the extent of his expert marksmanship. His aim was even more extraordinary considering the crudeness of his crossbow, which consisted of a short bow transfixed to a stock made from wood, with only a groove to guide the arrow [3]. A sear held Tell's string in the cocked position until he released it with the trigger [3].

What Tell needed to ease his nerves in shooting the apple was a modern convenience—a top-tier crossbow. Today's groundbreaking technology has led to significant improvements in the performance of crossbows, making shots more precise and faster, especially in comparison to weapons of the fourteenth century. Speed became an integral part of today's crossbows, with bows pushing arrows at 470 feet per second. This would've satisfied Tell, an archer with exceptionally high standards. He wouldn't have even once considered sacrificing form and accuracy to make up for shortcomings in speed. Benefiting from the high-efficiency features of today's bows, he'd have pulled less weight while still achieving respectable arrow speeds [4].

Nowadays, bows possess excellent string stretch, which is important when tuning a brand-new crossbow [4]. Surely, an avid hunter like Tell would've always kept his weapons well-tuned. Nevertheless, he wasn't expected to release 300 arrows in order to help the string stretch in the most advantageous manner. Bows these days produce zero stretch, which meant archers like Tell would've kept their bows in tune far longer. The lighter materials used in today's bows would've calmed Tell during his most dangerous shot of all time—considering they'd have increased his arrow's speed remarkably. A well-tuned bowstring would've offered Tell enhanced accuracy, and he wouldn't have broken a sweat as he targeted the precariously positioned fruit.

But the superior features in today's crossbows were only introduced as recently as the twenty-first century—700 years after Tell took the riskiest shot of his life. Improvements to the crossbows have been gradually made since the Middle Ages, when they were first utilized as leading missile weapons [3]. The crossbow was destructive even then, but it took on its most potentially devastating effects when the legendary Tell released his arrow into the center

105

of the apple on that poignant afternoon in the Swiss public square, becoming an unforgettable hero.

27

MONTEZUMA II AND THE CHOCOLATE BAR

Chocolate has a long and rich history, dating as far back as 1500 B.C.E. in Mesoamerica, when the Olmecs mixed cacao in their drinks. The delicious practice of drinking steaming, frothy chocolate during mealtimes spread to the Mayans around 600 B.C.E., when citizens of all social statuses enjoyed the chocolate beverage sweetened with honey, infused with vanilla from vanilla vines growing nearby, or—for a kick in the seat—spiced with chili peppers [1].

It wasn't until the Aztecs got wind of the custom of drinking chocolate that the cacao bean found its fame and glory. Since its beginnings in 1325 C.E., the Aztec Empire flourished. The Aztecs embraced the Mayan tradition of drinking chocolate and adopted it as their own, calling the drink Xocolatl and elevating chocolate to the status of a god. Chocolate was believed to have been sent to the Aztecs by none other than their serpent deity Quetzalcoatl. Drinking the delicate blend was reserved for wealthy priests, noblemen, and rulers, but the lower classes enjoyed a sip during weddings and celebrations [1]. The most renowned Aztec, Montezuma II, gulped chocolate by the gallons every day, believing it to be an instant energy drink and a reliable aphrodisiac—absolute necessities for a passionate emperor supporting two principal wives and hundreds of concubines.

While drinking chocolate lent the upper-class Aztecs plenty of merriment, it was the cacao bean that held the greatest value. Even gold failed to live up to the high worth of cacao beans. The highly regarded bean was traded alongside gold, turquoise, and cotton—and taxed. But the land under the Aztecs' feet couldn't support the growth of cacao trees, since the plants required a rich soil type, plentiful shade, and an abundance of humidity. Naturally, to acquire cacao beans, trade was essential. Cacao beans were used as currency, and swindlers mischievously counterfeited the precious beans. Instead of authentic cacao beans, unwitting Aztec victims curiously rolled small pebbles of clay on their outstretched palms [2].

The Spaniards learned of the Aztecs' wealth and invited themselves to the Valley of Mexico to meet Montezuma II. When Hernan Cortes asked for gold, legend has it that the Aztecs presented him with a basket full of cacao beans. Of course, Cortes accepted the beans and sent word back to Spain that they had discovered an earthly treasure that would sweeten the palate of the king, queen, and all the palace subjects. Indeed, the cacao bean did not fail.

But Montezuma II found himself in a pickle when Cortes' soldiers attacked. They focused on seizing the Aztec gold, as the emperor had accumulated stockpiles. The Aztec gold, some of it remaining mysteriously hidden after the various battles between the Spaniards and Aztecs, was rumored to be worth billions in today's money. Montezuma's warriors fought back, but the emperor and his empire ultimately fell at the hands of the Spanish [3].

Now, had Montezuma only known of a modern convenience—the recipe for solid chocolate bars—he'd have defeated the Spanish and reclaimed his empire. How could the simple chocolate bar have saved the Aztec Empire from annihilation? All the Aztecs had to do was take a lesson from the Trojans in 1184 B.C.E., when the Greek warriors built the gigantic Trojan Horse, hid forty warriors inside it and presented it as a gift to the enemy. Then, while the city slept, they snuck out, fought valiantly, and won the Trojan War.

The high-fat content in couverture chocolate gives it a high-ly moldable quality. Bars of solid chocolate could've been melted down, then sculpted into a myriad of forms, including larger-than-life giraffes. Had the Aztec warriors been fortunate enough to have known the recipe for producing modern chocolate, they'd have swiftly entertained the idea of melting massive amounts of choc-olate, molding it into a giant deity, such as Quetzalcoatl, then hid-ing warriors inside. Cortes would have proudly accepted the mon-umental chocolate gift. After all, he persuaded the Aztecs that he was a god. And of course, wouldn't Montezuma II have believed his claim? Why else could the Aztec emperor have the gall to present Cortes with a colossal gift made of the most valuable treasure in all of Mesoamerica?

Once Cortes lugged the giant chocolate sculpture back to camp with the Aztec warriors hidden inside, the Aztecs would have spec-tacularly jumped out and defeated the enemy—just as the Greeks had done during the Trojan War. The Night of Sorrows would nev-er have made history, and the Aztec Empire would've survived be-yond 1521 C.E.

Unfortunately for the Aztecs, solid chocolate wasn't invented until 300 years later in 1847 by the British chocolatier J.S. Fry and Sons. The delightful treat was concocted by blending sugar, co-coa butter, and chocolate liquor. Instead of drinking chocolate, as had been done for thousands of years, people of all social statuses dreamily bit down on solid bars of irresistible chocolate wrapped in shiny faux gold or silver foil. If only a modern convenience, like solid chocolate, had been invented three centuries sooner, 4,000 Aztec warriors, the Aztec Empire—and Montezuma II himself—would have survived to see another gleaming sunrise.

28

GALILEO GALILEI AND
THE EVENT HORIZON TELESCOPE

Over a thousand years ago, ancient cultures were bamboozled, believing the earth hovered at the center of the galaxy, encircled by the sun and other planets. Our blue planet was in a privileged position. As far back as the time of Aristotle, this geocentric theory was clear as daylight, since the earth showed no signs of constant movement: no hurling gusts of wind blew perpetually over the surface and no backward motions occurred when throwing an object up in the air—which would've been the case, if the earth were in motion [1].

The geocentric model of the universe had become entrenched in not only natural philosophy but religious doctrine [1]. The Catholic Church declared heresy when thinkers challenged geocentricism. But against the darkness of the night sky, ancient people saw the planets rotate position with their own eyes. These observations led to theorists, such as sixteenth-century Polish priest Nicolaus Copernicus, to assert that the earth was a planet like Venus, and that it rotated around the sun.

How dare he say the earth was just another insignificant planet in the vast, magnificent universe? Anyone who advanced the heliocentric theory could be punished by being burned at the stake, as was the unfortunate Italian scientist Giordano Bruno [1].

After the time of Copernicus, the heliocentric theory fascinated thinkers and spread. The telescope was first invented in 1608 by Hans Lippershey, a Dutch eyeglass craftsman [2]. His uncomplicated device magnified objects three times [2]. A year later, Galileo Galilei, enthralled upon hearing about the Dutch device, worked nonstop to produce a similar but enhanced version: one that magnified objects twenty times [2]. Galileo was the first to point his telescope toward the planets and stars pirouetting like ballerinas in the night sky.

What Galileo saw through his telescope was an unprecedented delight. He could see the deep craters in the moon and the ridges of mountains across its dry, dusty landscape [3]. Galileo turned his telescope to discover the shimmery pastel colors of Saturn's rings, then again to catch sight of a handful of Jupiter's moons [3]. Among the most surreal of his observations was the Milky Way, the sash of soft light holding steadfast across the darkened sky [3]. It was news to Galileo's contemporaries that our galaxy held countless shining stars.

As Galileo continued stargazing, he became increasingly convinced that Copernicus' heliocentric theory was astoundingly on target. The astronomer correctly observed the phases of Venus, which served as unwavering proof that the planets orbited the sun [3]. Did the nobleman dare oppose the Catholic Church with his evidence of the heliocentric model? After all, he could be blatantly charged with heresy.

But it was too late for the Florentine astronomer. Twenty-four years passed between Galileo first pointing his homemade telescope into the sky and being the target of Pope Urban VIII's inquisition [4]. In 1633, the physicist was ordered to surrender to the Holy Office and begin trial for his heretic belief that the earth spun like clockwork around the fiery sun [4]. Imprisonment and seclusion awaited Galileo. Ultimately, the Church pronounced their verdict: Galileo was guilty for believing the earth was not the center of the universe, and that the sun did not move from east to west [4]. Out of their will and pleasure, the Church sentenced Galileo to house arrest for the remainder of his life [4].

Now, had a modern convenience—the virtual telescope—been around 400 years ago, Galileo wouldn't have suffered misfortune for being a proponent of the heliocentric theory. The Event Horizon Telescope, EHT for short, was a groundbreaking technology that dissolved some of the mysteries of the universe, including the black hole in the center of the Milky Way. It took over 200 astronomers and scientists from around the world, plus the precise coordination of eight radio observatories, to create a virtual telescope that matched the size of the earth itself [5].

While Galileo's telescope could magnify distant objects twenty times, the magnification capable by the Event Horizon Telescope was mind-blowingly higher. In order to create a picture of a black hole, the telescope's magnification needed to be capable of, essentially, reading a lunch menu at a New York restaurant from an outdoor café in Paris. The largest, single radio telescope in the world doesn't have the magnification power to witness a shadowy black hole lingering fifty-five million light years away [5].

But the combination of multiple radio telescopes, from as far away as the Sierra Nevada to the Antarctic ice sheet, plus careful synchronization toward a single source in the sky, accomplished this astronomical feat [5]. It took the rare occasion of four clear nights, from the observatories scattered around the globe, to capture the image of a black hole in Messier 87, the scientific moniker for a galaxy inside the Virgo galaxy cluster [5]. Astrophysicists witnessed the fiery yellow-orange circle surrounding a dark shadow: the elusive black hole, never before photographed, and which is six-and-a-half billion times bigger than the sun around which our Earth spins [5].

The first picture of the black hole in Messier 87 was taken in 2019. A second picture was taken in 2022, when the Event Horizon Telescope captured the image of the supermassive black hole at the center of the Milky Way, boasting a mass of about four million suns—a good 152 quadrillion miles away from Earth [6]. Both were highly technological feats that would've knocked the silk hose stockings off Galileo's feet, confirming the accuracy of the heliocentric model and preventing him from living the rest of his productive life under restrictive house arrest.

Fortunately for astrophysicists today, theories about the unexplained universe are supported by the evolution of high-tech magnification devices, like the trusty virtual telescope that can photograph the black hole whirling at the center of our galaxy at the speed of light.

29

RAPHAEL SANZIO AND DIGITAL PAINTING

During the Italian High Renaissance in the sixteenth century, Raphael's shooting star briefly ascended the night sky. Unfortunately, his illustrious star plunged into unfathomable darkness before the stunned eyes of his contemporaries, robbing the world of a prolific master painter.

Raphael sped through life like a bullet train, working fervently and romancing salaciously. Although he died on his thirty-seventh birthday, his magnificent artistic career outlasted his brief lifespan, thanks to the prevalence of the artistic workshops of the period. Wealthy patrons yearned to possess the highly sought-after paintings by renowned artists like Raphael. No matter how remarkably endowed with unparalleled talent or genius, painters couldn't produce more art than was single-handedly possible by one person. And so was born the artistic workshop.

Inside these bustling artistic workshops, assistants flew back and forth, clasping the wooden handles of wet paintbrushes between their teeth and donning fashionable velvet berets that signaled to the art world that paintings of high caliber were at the cusp of being produced. The assistants' level of artistic skill varied. Some were students or apprentices. Others simply held the essential roles of workers [1]. Overseeing the entire operation was the lead painter, whose personal involvement in the paintings commanded greater desirability and increased their monetary value [1].

The benefits of running an artistic workshop were many. Raphael, and other painters in high demand, could satisfy the ongoing stampede of artistic commissions, thereby earning double than the average Florentine households in the sixteenth century [1]. To illustrate, Raphael was awarded nearly a thousand ducats for his altarpiece, *Santa Cecilia*, in 1514 [1]. Earning generous wages pushed successful Renaissance painters into the upper echelons of the artistic world.

Painters like Raphael weren't the only ones to benefit from the operation of workshops. Apprentices received invaluable artistic training [1]. A young Raphael himself was under the tutelage of Pietro Perugino, in whose workshop the emerging artist honed his artistic skills and earned his first commissions, among them being the *Marriage of the Virgin* in 1504 [1, 2]. The collaborations between the team lead and the apprentices proved formative in the latter's technique. The sheer volume of artistic output necessitated an exorbitant amount of help, and anyone who earned a position in the workshop was assured of being rewarded with a high degree of professional knowledge.

So it was unsurprising that, as demand for his paintings rose sharply in the sixteenth century, Raphael opened his own workshop in Rome [1]. He assembled a team of fifty qualified assistants, each offering a special skill, from expertise in stucco decorations to the ability to translate images into print [1, 3]. The artists in his network took Raphael's drawings and worked on them until the finished paintings met the high standards of the celebrated master painter. By serving as the head of his workshop, Raphael was able to supply powerful patrons with a steady stream of coveted paintings, artwork of significant worth because Raphael had a personal hand in their creations.

Of course, a moral question arose when obscure apprentices and assistants played influential parts in a piece of artwork that was ultimately attributed to a single painter. Raphael, whose natural talents deserved recognition, was credited with paintings of all ranks, from the small but rich frescoes in the Vatican papal housing to the world-famous *School of Athens*, a masterpiece of the High Renaissance. If Raphael hadn't completed works of art entirely himself, he designed them in complete independence.

Now, if only the highly sought-after Raphael had access to a modern convenience—digital painting software—he'd have released to the world an impressively inexhaustible oeuvre. Using computer software, a stylus, and a tablet, Raphael would've designed far more numerous pieces of art, then turned over the responsibility of finishing them to his pupils.

Holding the stylus like a brush, Raphael's students would've used the techniques they learned from their master and completed his paintings at warp speed. Since digital painting are finished faster than traditional paintings, this modern convenience would've met the tireless demands of Raphael's fastidious patrons. The quality of the digital paintings wouldn't have suffered, since styles of digital paintings mimicked those of traditional ones [4]. Styluses, for instance, could've convincingly represented oils, acrylic, or charcoal [4]. And if an assistant screwed up, he could've quickly deleted his mistake without having to return to Raphael, beg him to design an entirely new work, and risk arousing his ire. In the process, time and money spent on art materials would've been saved. Furthermore, Raphael wouldn't have needed to invest in the purchase of numerous easels, paintbrushes, palettes, and the space to house them all. Rather, the only supplies he'd have needed were the tablets for his pupils [4].

Clearly, by utilizing this modern convenience, Raphael would have fulfilled a greater number of artistic commissions in his few decades of life, thereby increasing his wealth and fame a thousand-fold. But digital painting did not arrive until the 1980's—over 400 years after Raphael's revered artistic contributions to the High Renaissance. The introduction of the personal computer made it possible for artists using digital painting to collaborate and share their work, which would've been an ideal situation in a sixteenth-century artistic workshop, where interactive learning was critical to growth.

Despite digital painting not having made its entrance in time nearly half a century ago, Raphael's work continued after his death. The altarpiece, the *Transfiguration*, was commissioned in 1517 but remained unfinished at Raphael's death in 1520 [2]. The master painter's assistant, Giulio Romano, however, completed the piece [2]. Similarly, Raphael continued to work beyond his grave with the Vatican's *Sala of Constantine*, not even begun until after his death [3]. Rather, Raphael's top students, including Giulio Romano, brought the painting to life based on their master's design [3].

Regardless of when digital painting was introduced, Raphael elevated art to subliminal heights. From his vibrant tapestries hung in the Sistine Chapel to his colorful frescoes to his sophisticated portraits and the feminine serenity he flawlessly captured in his Florentine Madonnas, Raphael was, and remains, one of the pre-eminent artists of all time. If only digital painting had been available in the sixteenth century, the world would've been far more beautified by the characteristic elegance and charm Raphael exuded not only through his personality but through a significantly greater number of his designs, which his pupils would've speedily finished. It wasn't for nothing, after all, that Raphael was known as the "prince of painters."

PART III: THE FLOURISHING YEARS

30

CIVIL WAR SOLDIER JAMES WINCHELL AND ANESTHESIA

Long before the introduction of modern anesthesia, pain was triggered by disease or injury and intensified to unimaginable heights by unrefined surgery. Egyptian medics crushed the mandrake root, extracting its juices and applying it as a surgical anesthetic as early as 1550 B.C.E. [1]. The ancient Egyptians conscientiously noted details of surgeries and other medical treatments on papyrus, the most well-known being the surviving Ebers Papyrus, a scroll unfolding to sixty-eight feet, comparable in length to the sauropod dinosaur Apatosaurus [1].

Ancient Roman surgeons preferred powdered opium, a drug also used to anesthetize patients in later Medieval times. Medical manuscripts from these periods indicated anesthetics prepared by mixing addictive opium, hallucinogenic mandrake juice, potentially deadly hemlock, and the all-around household staple, vinegar [2]. Patients in the Middle Ages fell unconscious when imbibing the brew, while the surgeons sliced them open in hopes of curing their painful ailment. The preferred painkiller in seventeenth-century Europe was a concoction of opium and the now highly controlled substance, laudanum (a blend of opium and high-proof alcohol). But because knowledge of anesthesia was barely in its infancy, surgeons found it difficult to administer the right doses. Hemlock could kill, as Socrates knew, and no one in their right mind wanted to become helplessly addicted to opium [2].

Because of the excruciating pain of surgery, procedures in earlier times were quick. Surgeries were deliberately performed swiftly and efficiently to not only minimize pain but reduce chances of infection—and the speed at which a surgeon could operate indicated his level of skill [3]. A surgeon earned a good reputation by amputating a thigh in under thirty seconds. Complicating the profession further, surgeons in the Middle Ages often held dual occupations: local barber and surgeon. After giving a young man a trendy bowl cut by flipping a cooking pot over his head and snipping the locks hanging below the rim, the barber would jet off to his surgical post, slicing up human flesh to remove a cyst or gallbladder stone. And due to ignorance of sanitization, it wasn't surprising when the medieval barber-surgeon used the same tool, unwashed, on both individuals.

Not too many early surgical procedures were performed before modern anesthesia, simply because no one wanted to bear the terrifying pain. Plus, surgery was incredibly risky when performed by surgeons who didn't attend four grueling years of medical school and spend an additional five-to-seven years training in surgical residency. Even dissecting amphibians to gain an understanding of anatomy was not common practice then. Slice it anyway you please, but early surgeons lacked sufficient surgical training—and the absence of modern anesthesia only worsened matters for everyone.

Indeed, patients weren't the only ones anticipating sheer horror upon going under the knife. Doctors, too, faced complex emotions as they gripped the scalpel in their quivering fist, while five or six physically agile assistants held down the screaming patient during the entirety of the operation [3]. If, at an inopportune moment, an assistant got in the way, the surgeon would accidentally cut off his finger—a health disaster in early times when antiseptics weren't available and infections could be fatal [3]. Further adding to the death toll of early operations were the unwitting onlookers who simply died of shock [3].

Improvements to pain management, from compressing nerves with tourniquets to hypnotizing surgical patients, spent but a brief time in the limelight. It wasn't until the mid-1800s that more promising solutions began to emerge. Ether could be vaporized and transformed into a colorless, sweet-smelling gas—one that numbed a patient's pain [3]. In 1846, ether was used to induce unconsciousness in a patient, while American dental surgeon William Morton painlessly removed the man's bulging neck tumor [3]. Two years later, another gas, chloroform, was proven to be effective in pain management.

But anesthesia was still in its primitive form during the American Civil War. As the battles between the Union and Confederate soldiers raged on from 1861 to 1865, the number of injuries mounted. Of the estimated 476,000 soldiers wounded, amputations were among the most common types of surgeries. Unluckily for Union Private James Winchell of the First United States Sharpshooters, his left arm was struck by a musket ball at the Battle of Gaines Mill. Only one surgeon treated the 500 prisoners captured, which included Winchell, who was forced to wait five days in agonizing pain before his injured arm was amputated—without anesthesia [4].

Winchell casually asked for a bottle of whiskey or a whiff of chloroform before the surgery [4]. After the soldier received a firm negative, the Civil War surgeon sliced Winchell's shoulder and removed the bone. Writhing and ready to die in the chair, Winchell insisted he didn't need the hour-long break the surgeon empathetically offered [4]. Admiring his spunk, the doctor determined he'd finish the job in the best way possible [4]. The stalwart soldier survived not only the battlefield surgery without the pain relief of whiskey, chloroform, or ether, but lived to tell his gutsy tale thirty years later.

It wasn't until another major war, World War II, that the gases used in modern anesthesia were developed. Out of the production of nuclear bombs in the 1930s came innovations in fluoridation chemistry that created safer anesthetics—specifically ones that wouldn't explode, like the highly flammable ether potentially could in gaslit, nineteenth-century operating rooms [3]. Rather than fearful patients being forcibly held down on the operating table, their physiology was continually and compassionately observed. Blood pressure, oxygen, carbon dioxide, and pulse were monitored by the equipment used in modern anesthesia, protecting patients' physical well-being.

Had only a modern convenience—modern anesthesia—been available to the remarkable Union Private James Winchell, he'd have suffered significantly less than he did on the open battlefield. It was enough that a lead musket ball tore through his tissue and shattered his bone, only for him to suffer capture by Confederate enemy soldiers. But having an arm amputated without anesthesia pushed his crushing misery over the top. Luckily for him, his natural spunk gave him the means to bravely endure his intolerable ordeal. Certainly, Winchell literally had the personal ammunition to boast of his harrowing but amazing once-in-a-lifetime Civil War story.

Since those shocking early days of rudimentary, inadequate pain relief, modern anesthesia has made major strides in recent decades, leaving patients with far less trepidation while outstretched on the cold, stainless steel operating table. Today, patients with a zest for life go so far as to eagerly join long waiting lists for elective surgery—an action completely unheard of before the days of modern anesthesia.

31

MAHATMA GANDHI AND SOCIAL MEDIA

Heralded as the Father of Modern India, Mahatma Gandhi was born in Porbandar in British India, in 1869. British rule over the subcontinent took hold eleven years prior, in 1858, and ceased in 1947 with Gandhi's influence. He lived to see his beloved country emancipated after a strenuous battle against foreign rule.

It was not an easy task to free India from the demoralizing grip of the British government. But Gandhi, educated as a lawyer, utilized the tools of the period to spread his views of nonviolent resistance to the masses. He favored the written word in newspapers to communicate with fellow Indians and non-Indians alike. This form of media was his most formidable tool in securing India's emancipation [1].

Over the course of forty years, Gandhi edited and published four newspapers [1]. *Indian Opinion*, his first publication, started in 1903, while he worked in South Africa [1]. Upon his return to India, he published his monthly newspaper, *Navajeevan* [1]. *Young India*, Gandhi's third publication, followed that same year in 1919 [1]. Unfortunately, due to British oppressiveness, *Young India* closed in 1932 [1]. Undeterred and behind bars for civil disobedience, Gandhi established *Harijan*, a weekly newspaper, in 1933 [1].

Through the many publications he edited and published, Gandhi expressed his views on nonviolence, self-reliance, self-rule, and truth—hoping to persuade, discuss, and debate current issues circling the nation [1]. For Gandhi, the articles in his newspapers were intended to motivate readers to take righteous action [1]. In his eyes, publishing was far from a source of income, but rather a noble service to his country [1]. He educated the masses on volatile subjects, including the equality of women, India's unfair caste system, prohibition, and the use of the spinning wheel as a means to generate supplemental income for the impoverished and unemployed Indians [1].

A powerful communicator, Gandhi roused the untapped sentiments of the masses, significantly growing a loyal following, especially during his many peaceful protests. The Salt March of 1930 proved to be a momentous nonviolent protest, where numerous Indians followed him to the sea to pick up salt, thereby breaking the British law that Indians must not produce salt [2]. The heavy salt tax levied by the British remained a contentious issue, beleaguering the majority of underprivileged Indians who could not afford to pay it [2]. In response, Gandhi organized a peaceful demonstration, where he walked 240 miles from western India to the coast of the Arabian Sea [2]. The dozen or so followers who initially accompanied him grew into larger and larger crowds as he passed through villages, railing against the unjustness of the salt tax [2].

Over the next couple months, Gandhi persuaded his followers to continue breaking the British law with an act of civil disobedience. Thousands of arrests and imprisonments followed [2]. Gandhi himself was detained, an act that spurred tens of thousands of Indians to join his campaign [2]. The Gandhi-Irwin Pact was eventually signed, which signaled the truce between Gandhi and Britain's Lord Irwin [2].

The Salt March was only one of Gandhi's successful acts of civil disobedience designed to free India from colonial rule. A decade later, Gandhi initiated another campaign called "Quit India," where he envisioned the United Kingdom voluntarily leaving India [3]. His message to his fellow citizens was clear: free India or die trying [3]. One thousand Indians perished at the hands of the British Army during the peaceful protests [3]. Despite the high cost of the protests, Gandhi's message rang loud and clear to the masses of Indians whose lives had been reduced to rubble as a direct result of deliberate British oppression. From 1942 to 1944, large numbers of Indians—from the nation's capital in Bombay to major cities in the south –engaged in peaceful protests, a strategy that ultimately led to India's freedom in 1947 [3].

Clearly, Gandhi's natural leadership ability united diverse populations. Now, if only he had access to a modern convenience—social media—he'd have had fared better in mobilizing the millions of India's citizens who grew weary of living under domineering British rule. His Salt March started out with only a dozen followers. But with a quick post to social media, Gandhi would've begun his long walk with thousands of people. How so? He'd have simply vented his ire about the unfairness of the salt tax on social media, which millions of Indians would've seen, then won them over with his sound logic, idealism, and patriotic love of his country. No doubt, Gandhi's social media posts would've instantly gone viral, thereby inspiring peasants even in the remotest villages to walk confidently by his side.

Gandhi's Quit India movement would've also communicated to the rest of the world the repressive activities of the British. The leader's social media posts would've been seen by people all over the globe. The aching starvation, miserable poverty, and loss of natural human freedoms imposed by the British would've escaped no one, as they'd all have been captured on video and shared multiple times over on various social media platforms. Attracting worldwide attention and outright disapproval, the British would've felt compelled to voluntarily exit India sooner than they did after World War II. Furthermore, rather than resort to newspapers to convey his ideals, Gandhi would've had at his fingertips the immense mobilizing power of social media. As Gandhi knew, newspapers could be quickly shut down by a British administration seeking to maintain the upper hand. The British, however, would've had a tougher time controlling the wide-ranging reach of social media.

But social media was not born until fifty years after India's independence, when the first platform was released. Countless social media sites have evolved since 1997, with just a handful of notable ones gaining worldwide traction [4]. The hashtags that arrived in 2007 would've organized all of Gandhi's posts, created ongoing awareness of India's valiant struggles, and helped drive further moral and political support from Japan, Italy, China, France, and the United States. Perhaps fewer Indians would've perished during the peaceful protests if social media posts vilified the violence and spurred action from powerful nations and allies. Even the rampant spread of disinformation and conspiracy theories on social media wouldn't have stopped a man as fiercely intelligent, resourceful, and persuasive as Gandhi. With a little help from social media, his peaceful role as the Father of Modern India would've played out far more smoothly, and he'd have rallied the world to accelerate India's independence.

32

NAPOLEON BONAPARTE AND
AI POSTURE CORRECTORS

Emperor of the French from 1804 until 1815, Napoleon Bonaparte cautiously shaped a public self-image of heightened power and grandeur. One remarkable painting of a gallant version of the general, *Napoleon Crossing the Alps*, was completed in 1801 to commemorate his success at the Battle of Marengo [1]. In this sublime depiction, Napoleon victoriously holds the reins of his majestic steed, his hair and cape billowing dramatically in the mighty mountain gusts blowing across the rocky ledge.

Napoleon was revered as an unmistakable French hero. He claimed more military victories than failures, and unsurprisingly won the confidence of the French people [1]. Though he grew up in unimpressive circumstances, he demonstrated that a stern will and exceptional intelligence, combined with military might, could accomplish anything—even assuming the role of emperor of France [1].

He was a believer in religious tolerance and freedom of conscience [1]. His Napoleonic Code gave life to these ideologies and more, including individual freedom and equality in the eyes of the law [1]. Napoleon, who emerged from the rubbles of a middle-class upbringing, made it easy for bourgeoisie men to enter the military [1]. Always a soldier, Napoleon strengthened his military with intents for the expansion of France beyond its borders. He entertained visions to reconquer Egypt and spread French influence in the Indian Ocean and the Mediterranean [1].

Throughout his great military achievements, Napoleon took firm hold of his reputation, commissioning a number of portraits of himself pictured as a dashing general and censoring the press whenever depictions of him teetered on ridicule. Even his coronation was intended to be exceptional. He wished for this extraordinary event to outdo those of other French sovereigns: the emperor wanted to be consecrated by the pope himself [1]. Insecure and impatient, Napoleon did what he's most known for today—he seized the crown from the pope's hands, set the bejeweled piece on his own head, and proclaimed himself emperor of France.

The touchy emperor was known for his bold moves. Rather than impress his opponents, they lathered on the criticism. In 1803, France was still battling Great Britain. Tall and elegant, British soldiers made the French look diminutive. In fact, Napoleon was nicknamed La Petit Caporal, or Little Corporal, but not for his stature. It was instead a term of endearment given to him by his soldiers [2]. Napoleon also wore his brunette locks cropped and short, which earned him the moniker La Petit Tondu, or Little Crop-Head [1]. *Little* seemed to be a common thread throughout the life of the great emperor of France.

Napoleon may indeed have been a small individual, thought to have been standing between five-foot-two inches and five-foot-seven inches tall—an average height range for a nineteenth-century Frenchman [2]. But his British enemies played down his average stature by wielding the power of political cartoons. Starting with caricatures of Napoleon being childish and throwing temper tantrums, the cartoons progressed to simply depicting him as short [2]. Tickled, the public lapped it up. And the portrayal stuck.

The insecure emperor, however, was far from amused. His public image had been carefully cultivated over the years, and the

British cartoonists took it upon themselves to mock it with irreverent joy. The emperor's first wife, Josephine, loomed in height over the wee Napoleon in the British press. In popular cartoons of the day, Napoleon stood half as tall as his troops, which may have been an exaggeration of the truth, considering British soldiers were indeed significantly taller than French ones [2].

Despite his many military accomplishments, Napoleon was thin-skinned. Perhaps due to his humble beginnings, he carried with him a lifelong insecurity. And who else but Napoleon would break from centuries of tradition to brazenly crown himself emperor? Given the combination of his inferiority complex, his lack of a sense of humor, and his renown, Napoleon was highly worthy of ridicule—and the press did not disappoint. The French emperor felt so distraught being mocked for his height that he attempted to censure the British press. Of course, he failed magnificently, and the cartoonists naturally lampooned him further.

Whether or not Napoleon was truly short, he was reputed to be. In the oil painting *The Emperor Napoleon in His Study* at the Tuileries, his right hand was famously tucked into his vest. The emperor indeed took on the appearance of a stocky and diminutive individual. He may have been of average height for men of his place and time, but he undoubtedly wanted to appear as a towering height of power and glory. Any power-hungry man would jump at the chance to show overarching influence purely through imposing physical height.

Now, had Napoleon only had access to a modern convenience—the AI posture corrector—he'd have circumvented the ridicule that brought him such gloom. The emperor would've optimized his height potential by improving his slouch with this handy little (or, shall we say, La Petit?) device. Whenever he'd hunched, as he did in his portrait of himself in his study, the AI posture corrector would've given him a slight vibrating jolt, reminding him to stand as tall as the daring, accomplished general he was. The AI posture corrector would've been hardly noticeable, taking the form of a small rectangle adhered discreetly to his back. He could've worn his handsome military uniform over it, and the observant British cartoonists would've been none the wiser.

Napoleon could've tracked his habit of unhappy slouching—which he had the liberty to do after he was defeated and exiled in 1815, but not a minute before—and seen just how bad his habit really was. The built-in sensor that detected movement would've provided him with humbling data over the course of a week, which he could've used to course correct, and he'd only have to recharge the battery every two-and-a-half days [3]. The preset angles on the AI posture corrector could've been adjusted to befit the image of an accomplished emperor, which would've been as tall and dignified as possible. But if Napoleon were lazy, which he certainly wasn't, he'd have easily left the device preset.

Of course, Napoleon could've experimented with posture exercises and yoga to improve his height [4]. Performing the mountain pose, or child's pose, could've given him the look of an intimidatingly tall general, worthy of public admiration and not a word of mockery. Modern conveniences, though, would have made the whole endeavor much easier, and involved less hard work.

But AI posture correctors were released only in the twenty-first century—over 200 years after the trail-blazing era of Emperor Napoleon. He was destined to suffer the reputation of being a comically short French emperor for the duration of his fifty-one years and forever afterward, simply because AI posture correctors weren't around to help him stand habitually, proudly tall.

33

ALBERT EINSTEIN AND PERFORMANCE SOCKS

Genius is uncommon, almost as rare as socks that never develop holes in the roomy toe area. An intelligence quotient must hover around 180 to qualify as the ultimate genius [1]. According to this criterion, genius pops up once in every two million people [1]. Genius is defined in numerous ways, including heightened creativity, an abundance of originality, and the ability to think in unusual yet highly constructive ways—like intentionally circumventing sock-wearing, when the disadvantages clearly outweigh the advantages [1].

One eminent genius was a German-born physicist named Albert Einstein. His notable work in physics earned him the prestigious Nobel Prize for Physics in 1921. As a child, he was fascinated by invisible forces, such as what moved the needle of a compass, the principles of geometry, and the unsolvable conundrum of what might happen upon racing a light beam [2].

His preoccupation with the speed of light, however, gave him his claim to fame. Einstein's theory of relativity didn't win him the Nobel Prize, but he instead won the award for his ideas on the photoelectric effect [2]. Einstein also proposed that the universe was expanding or contracting, and refrained from the universal belief at the time that the universe was static [2]. Clearly, he didn't acquiesce to popular views—like that of always donning a pair of good socks.

Einstein received numerous invitations to speak about his ideas. Everywhere he went, audiences numbered in the thousands, eager to catch a glimpse of the man with the mane of eccentric hair who rattled off profound ideas about everything that made the universe tick. During one visit to California, the actor Charlie Chaplin remarked that audiences applauded him, Chaplin, because everyone understood him, while audiences applauded Einstein because no one understood him [2]. Einstein rubbed shoulders with many other notable professionals, including psychoanalyst Sigmund Freud and Indian poet Rabindranath Tagore. Unknown to his swooning audiences, during each event, he went sockless.

A man of ideas, Einstein held in-depth talks with his associates on subjects, like physics, religion, and politics [2]. During his walks around Princeton, he dressed comfortably for the occasion: baggy trousers, an undershirt, and sandals. He felt unusual pride in not wearing socks whenever he gave lectures at Oxford. In fact, Einstein was notorious for never wearing socks. He simply hated them.

Einstein's rationale for never wearing socks had its roots in a childhood invested in mathematics and physics. His big toe loomed longer than the rest of his toes, and the behemoth frequently tore a gaping hole in the fabric [3]. And everyone knows that wearing socks with a massive hole in the toe is highly uncomfortable.

The sign of a true genius is to immediately put an end to any habit causing discomfort, and Einstein did not fail in this regard. Aside from his theory of relativity, which elevated his professional reputation, Einstein was known for a quirk: he'd didn't wear socks, simply because of the holes that appeared as a result of his mischievous big toe.

He even declined an offer to serve as president of Israel, a largely ceremonial role that required a prim and proper appearance from head to toe [4]. Einstein's reasoning for his rejection of the proposal was based on his lifetime of work dealing with the objective, rather than with the subjective whims of people, of which he had little experience [4]. Looking deeper, it was likely that Einstein didn't own an elegant pair of socks, which would have been an important piece of attire vital for one officiating numerous international political affairs. Plus, in such a high-profile role, he couldn't disguise his socklessness by wearing high boots, as he often did [4].

Now, what Einstein needed was a modern convenience—contemporary performance socks—to keep his toes well-cushioned no matter where he traveled. If he'd worn a pair of well-made socks, he'd have attended dinner parties without fearing that his naughty big toe would boldly push through the tip of his socks. A durable pair of performance socks would've made his walks around Princeton a comfortable occasion, wear after wear. His best pair of durable socks would've endured for over a decade.

Socks made from high-density knitting would've been especially durable. In this special type of knit, several needles created tiny stitches, making it less likely that Einstein's big toe would have punctured through the tip of the sock. Resistance to tears increased when socks were manufactured using different fibers and various stitches [5]. In this regard, merino wool would've been the ideal material with which to manufacture the most durable socks. Merino fibers were valued for their ability to stretch without losing elasticity and breaking [5]. When merino wool was used in combination with nylon and spandex yarn, a natural resilience emerged. Not even Einstein's big toe would've broken through the tensile strength of socks made with such high-quality materials.

The sock-dodging Einstein could've counted on socks reinforced from the outside with nylon and, on the inside, cushioned with reinforcements. He could've walked for miles and miles all over the Princeton campus and never once felt the need to complain about a hole in the toe of his sock. Plus, given his fame, he would've enjoyed custom-made socks, designed to be a perfect fit, even accommodating his big toe that stuck out farther than the rest. A better fitting sock lasted longer. Unlike the effortlessness with which his theory of relativity came to him, it'd have taken Einstein a great deal of work to put a hole in durable performance socks.

Climate-wise, Einstein would've readily adapted to the frigid New Jersey winters by wearing performance socks with thermo-regulating features. Even the hottest summer days would've been noticeably pleasant on his feet. If it did get unbearably hot, the moisture-wicking powers of merino wool would've absorbed the dampness, leaving his feet dry and comfy.

Though socks have been worn since 1500 B.C.E., high-performing lifestyle socks are a modern convenience. Einstein may have been a thinker ahead of his time, but his feet certainly deserved better. Little did Einstein know the luxury he was missing. If only he'd had access to today's durable, thermoregulating, moisture-wicking, odor-resistant performance socks, he might've reconsidered sock-wearing and eased into his deep highbrow discussions with enhanced comfort.

34

FRANKENSTEIN NOVELIST MARY SHELLEY AND DICTATION SOFTWARE

Long drizzly nights stuck indoors in the company of three vacationing friends prompted Mary Wollstonecraft Shelley to pen one of the most famous novels, *Frankenstein, or The Modern Prometheus*, better known to contemporary popular culture as *Frankenstein*.

Shelley was a refined, well-educated eighteen-year-old woman, head-over-heels-in-love with fellow writer and poet, Percy Bysshe Shelley, whom she eventually wed [1]. An immediate hit when it was published, *Frankenstein* combined elements of gothic literature with moral philosophy, yet found a homey place within the emerging genre of science fiction [2].

Frankenstein took life over the course of a few stormy evenings in 1816 at a villa near Lake Geneva in Switzerland [1]. Traveling with her lover Percy Bysshe Shelley, Mary Shelley visited their mutual friend, Lord Byron, another accomplished poet of the Romantic era. Fortunately for literature, the rainy Swiss weather was far from ideal to accommodate the friends' plans to pursue outdoor activities [1]. The group cozied up around a fire at Byron's villa, entertaining themselves with readings of ghost stories [1].

An idea struck like the sound of thunder, and Byron suggested they all compete in writing a ghost story. Writhing with anxiety, the eighteen-year-old Shelley battled writer's block before she even put a single word to paper. She couldn't invent a ghost story for the life of her. The close friends nevertheless began a round of discussions about the ethics of life. During these discussions, the tiny flicker that would grow to the monstrous fire of *Frankenstein* ignited in Shelley's imagination.

Sheltered from the ominous clouds, clapping thunder, and the torrential rain, she proposed to her companions the idea of reanimating a human corpse [1]. Shelley ran with the heart of her story after being besieged with a conscious dream of an experimental corpse stretched out in a lab, then being shocked awake with the gift of life—and the instinct to bring death and destruction.

Shelley started her story in Switzerland, then fleshed it out into a full novel in England [1]. Using a quill pen, she scribbled feverishly about the moonlight escapades of her man-made monster. Every inch of beige paper in her elegant notebook became filled with handwritten words, some hastily crossed out and replaced with more fitting descriptors. At times, entire sentences were wiped out or added in the margins. Shelley proved herself to be a talented debut novelist, but her handwriting was a terrible ordeal to decipher.

It was 1818 before the first edition of *Frankenstein* was published anonymously [1]. A second edition followed, this time with Shelley credited as the author [1]. Shelley was twenty when her novel fell into the hands of the enchanted public. And it became an instant hit.

Shelley's 75,000-word novel took a few short nights to conceive and two long years to write. Surely, this natural-born storyteller knew her sordid characters and inventive plot inside and out before she set out to write it all down. What primarily occupied her was the amount of time and stamina it took to handwrite, and revise, every single word.

What she needed was a modern convenience—dictation software—to help her bring her story to life in the same intrepid manner that the mad scientist in her famous novel capriciously brought the morbid but endearing Frankenstein to life. Rather than spend months writing at her desk, Shelley would've used dictation software to speak her story into her phone, all while telling her vivid story to her three attentive friends, and watched the typewritten words automatically appear on her screen. Instantly, her story would've been ready for the publisher and the printer.

All those stormy summer nights inside Byron's elegant villa would've felt more deliciously haunting, had Shelley spoken her accounts of the tortured Frankenstein, her dictation software running silently in the background, capturing every philosophical nugget and gothic detail.

Writing novels in the nineteenth century was grueling work, especially when every word had to be handwritten legibly and meticulously to be read by publishers and nineteenth-century printers. Dictation software would've produced clean text in classic Blackletter typeface. Relying on dictation software, she'd have avoided the risk of gradually destroying her wrists with carpal tunnel syndrome, and reducing any potential back pain from hunching over her desk scribbling away for two years until the wee hours of each morning. Shelley could've even taken her story outside, embellishing her story and troubled characters under the protection of a weather-proof canopy, since dictation software can be used virtually anywhere.

And with Shelley coming from a wealthy family of well-recognized English writers, including her father William Godwin, she'd have easily been able to afford the cost of dictation software. Regardless, her one-time investment in the purchase of the software would've paid her back handsomely, considering she went on to author many more books, including *The Last Man* in 1826, *The Fortunes of Perkin Warbeck* in 1830, and *Falkner* in 1837. Shelley could've continued relying on her trusty and accurate dictation software as she heavily revised *Frankenstein* for the popular edition published in 1831, which is the version of Shelley's novel widely read today.

But dictation software wasn't invented until 1990—over 150 years after the release of *Frankenstein*. What a time-saving, health-preserving boon dictation software would've been to nineteenth-century writers, who relied on peak physical endurance and immense mental fortitude to breathe life into the fantastical stories begging to escape their imaginations.

35

GIOACHINO ROSSINI AND TRUFFLE BURGERS

Early nineteenth century music enamored audiences as equally as the era's fine food, thanks to Italian composer Gioachino Rossini. As a young boy, he was surrounded by music from his trumpeter father and his singer mother [1]. The theater was Rossini's second home during his carefree childhood of laziness and leisure [1]. Singing and learning to play music came as easy as French silk pie to him [1]. By the age of fifteen, the future composer had learned the violin, harpsichord, and horn [1]. He soon graduated to the roles of accompanist and conductor [1].

Within a span of twenty years, Rossini composed over forty operas, his specialty being the comic opera. He was famous, and sometimes mocked, for his prolific use of the crescendo [1]. His operas included *Elizabeth, Queen of England* in 1815 and *The Barber of Seville* in 1816. *Othello* soon followed, and later *The Thieving Magpie*— all triumphant successes for the Italian composer. Rossini proudly proclaimed that *The Barber of Seville* took him only three weeks to complete. *William Tell*, Rossini's final opera, was finished before he retired to his villa in Passy, near Paris, France.

Comfortable at his villa, Rossini threw elaborate gourmet dinners consisting of his favorite foods: foie gras, truffles, and cheese [2, 3]. His guests included the most notable musicians of the day, including German composer Richard Wagner, who praised the great Rossini in his essay "A Memory of Rossini" [1]. While entertaining, Rossini showed off his quick wit, philosophizing about the glories of food as passionately as the wonders of music [3]. With utter sincerity, Rossini said that "appetite is for the stomach what love is for the heart," and he compared the four acts of a comic opera to "eating, loving, singing and digesting" [3].

Among his dinner guests was his close friend, a chef who had dedicated elaborate recipes to Rossini [4]. Returning the affable gesture, Rossini wrote piano pieces about his friend's entrees and desserts [4]. He'd joke with his guests that it took him only four minutes to compose an aria [5]. Writing came so effortlessly to Rossini that he was happy to simply set even laundry lists to music [5].

Rossini was a talented gentleman, composing not only brilliant comic operas but creating culinary masterpieces. If he didn't have a hand in personally preparing a delicious entrée, he enjoyed such a gregarious personality that one was created specifically in his honor [2]. It wasn't uncommon to come across gourmet recipes bearing the name à la Rossini [2].

Although Rossini retired from writing comic operas, he continued composing the occasional musical pieces about his other passion: food. His compositions ranged from pieces about mundane tidbits, from raisins and nuts to anchovies and cornichons [3]. He could compose a riveting piece of music about anything under the sun—as long as it fancied his epicurean tastes.

Now, knowing Rossini savored fine meals enough to compose music about their delectable ingredients, it would've been unsurprising had he written about a modern convenience—the truffle burger. Since he could set to music such commonplace things as laundry lists and raisins, it'd have been no wonder if he had likewise set balsamic-glazed mushrooms, Swiss cheese, truffle aioli, and an all-meat patty to music just as magnificently. It'd have taken him four minutes to write a spectacular aria about the truffle burger. He'd probably have written a multitude of spellbinding arias within a short span of twenty minutes, celebrating variations of the burger, from white truffle burgers to black truffle burgers, some layered with Havarti cheese, others with melted Swiss.

But the truffle burger was unveiled only in the twenty-first century, several decades after the original hamburger was introduced to a world ravenous for a pairing of meat and bread. In fact, the creation of the first true hamburger was credited to Charlie Nagreen, affectionately known as "Hamburger Charlie," in 1885 at the Seymour Fair in Wisconsin [6]. Nagreen wanted to give customers strolling around the fair the opportunity to simultaneously walk and eat, so he stuffed beef meatballs between two slices of bread, and claimed it as the first hamburger. The creation of the all-beef patty sandwiched between a sourdough bun eventually led to its own holiday: National Birth of the Hamburger Day—a special day to which Rossini would've naturally dedicated a riveting musical piece.

If only the truffle burger had been introduced during Rossini's lifetime in the early nineteenth century, he'd have relished this exquisite meal like only a true connoisseur would, all while composing delightful music to express his undying love for the beef and bread combo. The truffle burger, after all, was built with ingredients Rossini cherished most: truffles, truffle sauce, and more truffles. The burger also contained a hefty slice of truffled goat's cheese, which would've satisfied Rossini's indulgent taste buds like nothing else on earth. Unfortunately for his discerning gastronomic appetite, Rossini didn't live to see the invention of either the hamburger or the truffle burger. He died in 1868 at his villa in Passy, without ever having the chance to sample a truffle burger that would have tasted as deliciously spirited to the tastebuds as *William Tell* sounded to the musically refined ear.

36

BRITISH FACTORY WORKERS AND
DIGITAL ALARM CLOCKS

The industrial revolution introduced machinery to rapidly produce goods once made painstakingly by hand. Mechanized
processes, steam, and steel grew to be pivotal forces in grand scale
manufacturing. Mass production paved the way for the sale of
cheaper goods, establishing instant demand for a sea of factories.

Factories popped up all over England. Scores of British people
flocked to the cities to be closer to the factories and search for work
[1]. Initially, at the start of the eighteenth century, 10,000 inhabitants lived in the small village of Manchester [1]. By 1801, Greater
Manchester had ballooned into a bustling city of over 300,000 people, and by mid-century, the population skyrocketed to over one
million [1]. Similarly, London was a crowded city of one million in
1801 [1]. The next year its population doubled, and by 1891, London
found itself managing the residential needs of almost six million
inhabitants [1].

Hundreds of people worked inside England's factories [2].
Working conditions inside the manufacturing plants were inex-
cusably poor, with dust and heat triggering major health concerns.
Fast-moving machinery and overcrowded environments made factories highly dangerous, especially for children [2]. These diminutive, underage workers—sent from orphanages—were forced to

crawl through tight spaces between factory equipment [2]. Needless to say, accidents happened frequently. Factory owners contributed to the prison-like environments, enforcing harsh discipline and overworking employees [2]. It wasn't uncommon for factory workers to grind away for twelve hours a day [2].

Conditions inside factories were dismal. Nevertheless, factory workers still woke up early to head to work and earn their twenty-five shillings per week. British workers didn't have many other viable options, if they wanted to earn a living. But in order to get up at the crack of dawn, they needed a reliable way to be roused out of their restful nighttime slumber. Mechanical alarm clocks were beyond the budget of factory workers; plus, alarm clocks were notorious for malfunctioning. The next best solution was the career-minded knocker upper. Carrying a long stick, these professionals rapped at the windows of their customers, waking them from their sleep.

Like factory workers, knocker uppers didn't work for free. They charged a nominal sum to wake up their clients in time for their day's work. Typically, a knocker upper would earn six pence per week, per client [3]. Knocker uppers were peculiar-but-familiar sights in England's northern mill towns, where the majority of the factories were built [3].

Knocker uppers commonly used long poles, as well as pea shooters, soft hammers, and rattles [3]. The key was for the knocker uppers to awaken their paying client, but not the unpaying neighbors next door [3]. It'd have been bad for business to wake people for free. And so the knocker uppers devised an inventive strategy: they modified their poles, so that only their clients would be awoken but not their non-paying neighbors [3]. Plus, the knocker uppers wouldn't linger for too long; a few taps to jostle a client would've been sufficient, and off they'd go to knock against the next window [4]. Several dedicated knocker uppers were keen on customer satisfaction, so they waited below until they were certain their client was awake.

The cushiony job grew into a popular trade across England [3]. If a factory shift began at six in the morning, the knocker upper would be sure to tap at the client's window by five o'clock. A tardy knocker upper meant their clients would oversleep, be late to work, lose valuable pay, and ultimately be unable to pay the knocker upper's weekly wage. The best knocker uppers were prompt and professional.

But the big question was, who woke up the knocker upper? And, who woke up the knocker upper who woke up the knocker upper? It's a question that went around and around in circles with no clear answer. It may help to know the knocker uppers kept unusual hours. They normally slept during the day, awakening around one in the morning in order to perform their daily responsibilities [3]. The knocker uppers hobbled along the cobblestone streets, snugly wrapped in a cozy shawl to protect themselves against the English chill and dampness. A beloved pet dog might've accompanied the knocker uppers as they gingerly rapped at the windows of clients. They even retired after a long, well-respected career.

Knocker uppers enjoyed long-term work, from the 1800s until the 1940s and 1950s, when their profession gradually died out [3]. Electricity and functional alarm clocks became prevalent, eliminating the need for factory workers to pay for the knocker uppers' services [3].

Factory workers in England received pay, but only enough to pay a knocker upper six pence weekly. Plus, in rainstorms, it'd have been nigh impossible for factory workers to differentiate three to four deliberate taps on their windows from the onslaught of pelting raindrops. For this reason, during storms, factory workers were likely to have overslept, and what compassionate human would've asked an elderly knocker upper to brave the fierce morning storms? Indeed, though popular, the knocker upper wasn't a hundred percent reliable in England's adverse weather conditions.

Furthermore, knocker uppers must have been disadvantaged when trying to wake heavy sleepers. A few raps on the window wouldn't have awoken hardy workers who'd been drinking all night, or who'd fallen naturally into a deep slumber. Usually, the knocker upper would've tapped at the window facing the street, so those who slept in the back bedroom wouldn't have heard the taps at the front of the house. There was also the risk that, once awakened by a knocker upper, a factory worker would roll back to sleep and make himself late. These professionals didn't offer extra snooze services. Under circumstances like these, knocker uppers wouldn't have been useful to factory workers.

Indeed, nineteenth-century factory workers needed the digital alarm clock. While factory workers weren't paid enough to even buy their own watches, a digital alarm clock would've been inexpensive, even by the economic standards of early nineteenth-century factory workers [3]. It would've operated despite the weather, and blared loud enough to wake even the heaviest of sleepers.

Factory workers wouldn't have slept through the buzzing sounds produced by the digital alarm clock. They wouldn't have kept rolling back to sleep after hitting the snooze button and hearing the alarm go off again nine minutes later. British factory workers who refused to be jolted awake by a jarring alarm would've enjoyed plenty of other options, such as the musical chirps of birds or the calming sounds of a babbling river. An auditory digital alarm would've suited many factory workers just fine.

Then there were those who'd have enjoyed nothing better than to be awoken by the soft glow of sunlight. A sunrise digital alarm clock would've gradually and peacefully eased factory workers from their slumber. Since the alarm clock light would've mimicked sunlight, waking up would've been quite a pleasant experience [5]. Although a sunrise alarm clock would've been more expensive than a standard digital alarm clock, factory workers of the period would've made a smart move by purchasing one. Their investment would've not only reliably woken them up in time to prepare for work, but improved their quality of sleep [5]. A refreshed factory worker would've been alert on the job, thereby avoiding perilous workplace accidents. A digital alarm could've potentially saved a nineteenth-century factory worker's life.

But it took over a century since the knocker uppers first appeared before the digital alarm clock was patented, in 1956. In 1970, a more advanced digital alarm clock entered the market and versions of it evolved to become mainstream. Thanks to digital alarm clocks, no one is compelled to rely on three or four dubious raps on their window in order to wake for the workday.

37

MARILYN MONROE AND
FOOD DELIVERY SERVICES

Electrifying on the silver screen, Marilyn Monroe was acclaimed for her wide-eyed innocence as much as her voluptuous curves. While it was clear that she entertained millions of fans who watched her sizzle in the greatest movies of the 1950s, the real question was, could she entertain a guest or two with sizzling lamb chops and a steak from her kitchen?

Little did Marilyn Monroe's emotionally unstable mother, Gladys Pearl Baker, know that she'd just given birth to a daughter who'd become the most unforgettable pop culture icon of her time. Originally Norma Jeane Mortenson, Marilyn Monroe flaunted her scraggly curls in photos with extended family and friends. No matter who else posed in these candid photos, Marilyn's magnetic persona captured every drop of attention.

In a 1944 professional photo that launched her career, the eighteen-year-old wore her signature painted smile as she showed off a metallic propeller from a pilotless aircraft at the Radioplane defense plant [1, 2]. A year later, her frizzy red hair was toned down to sleek perfection for an early modeling shoot [3].

The blossoming twenty-one-year-old signed with 20th Century Fox and assumed the name Marilyn, a popular feminine name at the time, and Monroe, her mother's maiden name. The young starlet trained long hours with acting coaches to hone her craft, reading books on drama, art, and psychology, and winning praise from audiences and critics for small roles in dramas [1]. Now blond but still projecting a smile overflowing with natural charm, Monroe shone as the epitome of glamour.

It wasn't until the 1950s that Monroe's unwavering dedication to her craft hurled her to international stardom. The grand Niagara Falls and the charismatic Monroe—both making splashes on the silver screen—competed on equal footing for the attention of film audiences in the 1953 film *Niagara*. In the same year, Monroe also proved to the world that blonds do have more fun, sporting diamonds in *Gentlemen Prefer Blondes*.

When she appeared at the *Gentlemen Prefer Blondes* film premiere with world-class actors, Monroe's bubbly personality was incandescent. She left not only her handprints in the cement outside Grauman's Chinese Theater in Los Angeles, but a lasting impression of unstoppable joy. Dressed from head to toe in quintessential Hollywood style, she signed autographs for fans young and old alike. Even as a newlywed married to Joe DiMaggio in 1954, Monroe's fizz didn't die down. She was a public persona, basking in global adoration.

An actress with extraordinary range and comedic timing, Monroe was just as formidable in the kitchen. Though she spent little time at home, her hotel room served as her makeshift residence during the heydays of her ascending career. Monroe's eighteen hours on set kept her busy. Still, she managed to consume an adequate supply of nutrients to maintain her energy and health. It also didn't hurt that a slather of Vaseline helped maintain her youthful glow [4].

Monroe was never one to give her slender figure much thought [5]. Instead, she worried about getting enough nourishment to sustain her during the strenuous days on the film set [5]. Breakfast was deceptively simple: two raw eggs cracked into a glass of warm milk

[5]. A multivitamin supplemented her eggnog-like morning beverage [5]. She was the first to profess that no doctor could recommend a healthier way to start the day—and she couldn't have been more correct [5].

Surprisingly, the starlet spent her evenings dining in. After putting in long hours on set, she'd stop by the local market for a single-sized portion of lamb chops, liver, or good old-fashioned steak [5]. Just as Monroe was a natural in front of the camera, she exuded effortlessness in the kitchen. Her hotel room didn't afford her an extravagant stove or oven, but it did provide her with an electric oven [5]. She'd season her daily protein, then broil it to perfection. A few raw carrots, which she never tired of eating, served as a vitamin-packed side dish [5]. And that was the gist of her nightly dinners.

As Monroe was an actress in high demand with little time to cook, she'd have benefitted from the ease of modern-day food delivery services. All she had to do was open the app on her smartphone, search for a particular kind of food—in this case lamb chops or steak—and she'd instantly have been shown a slew of important information, from delivery fees to delivery times. The actress would've simply had to navigate to her choice of restaurant and place her order. Monroe spent most of her time in densely populated urban areas, so she'd have enjoyed receiving her food three times faster than if she'd ordered from a remote suburban location.

Since Monroe was keen on protein, she would've felt exuberant about the rewards programs built into the best food delivery apps. If she ordered lamb chops three times, she'd have received a credit on her next order. Every little bit saved was worth the trouble for an actress who was paid ten times less than her co-star Jane Russell in *Gentlemen Prefer Blondes* [6].

It's a given that Monroe forgot mechanical techniques while in front of the camera, so she'd often miss her mark [4]. But the robust features in food delivery apps would've made her forgetfulness a trivial matter. In the event Monroe enjoyed a sumptuous

149

meal from a restaurant but forgot its name, she could've quickly navigated back to her prior orders and simply tapped to reorder.

Some choice food delivery apps would've given Monroe the ability to order not only food, but the makeup she relied on to accentuate her most attractive features, plus a range of pet supplies. As a pet parent to several beloved dogs throughout her lifetime, including a Maltese terrier nicknamed Maf, Monroe would've appreciated the convenience right at her fingertips [6].

But food delivery services didn't soar to popular heights until 2018, when customers ordered $10.2 billion worth of meals [7]. Food delivery services had been in business since 2011, though, and steadily expanded their services nationally and internationally over the years [7]. Monroe could've ordered a favorite protein-rich meal from anywhere in the world, if the handy app had been available then, instead of emerging fifty years after her last film, *The Misfits*. Food delivery, like many aspects of society, has been altered significantly by technology. But Monroe's recipes for tender lamb chops and broiled steak persevere.

38

THEODORE ROOSEVELT AND THE FREEZER

Few people in history lived so fully and vigorously that no modern convenience could've enhanced their quality of life. Theodore Roosevelt was such a remarkable individual. On record, he stated that no one had ever "led a happier life" than he [1]. And how true he showed it to be! Yet despite Roosevelt making good use of life's every trapping or unanticipated twist and turn, each historical persona could've benefited somewhat from the modern conveniences afforded to us today.

Born to a wealthy New York family in 1858, Roosevelt grew up privileged yet sickly with asthma [2]. As a young man, he attended Harvard College, then pursued legal studies at Columbia Law School. But politics gave him a stronger calling, and he left law school without graduating. At the age of twenty-three, he won a Republican seat in the New York State Assembly.

In due time, he found himself serving as Vice President to President William McKinley. Roosevelt proved himself a powerful military leader, as evidenced by his courageous leading of the famed Rough Riders during battles in the Spanish-American War. When President McKinley was assassinated, Roosevelt, then forty-two, became the youngest ever to be sworn in as President of the United States.

Roosevelt made great strides as president, involving the US in aggressive foreign policy measures. He was the first US president to win the Nobel Peace Prize for helping to negotiate peace between Japan and Russia [3]. The US Forest Service was created as a result of Roosevelt's influence [2]. The president was a staunch conservationist, and established nearly 200 million acres of public land as national forests [2]. He held a lifelong admiration for nature, a quality he developed while herding cattle at his Dakota ranch.

Even as an active president, Roosevelt did not relinquish his love for hunting. He enjoyed numerous hunting trips, the most famous of which occurred in 1902 in the Mississippi wilderness. Roosevelt's guide had tied a bear to a tree, making it an easy target for the president. Valuing sport over ease, Roosevelt refused to shoot the bear [3]. Cartoonists got wind of his merciful deed and spread news of it through political cartoons. A shopkeeper saw the cartoons and chose to name his line of stuffed bears after him. Thus, the beloved teddy bear was born [3].

To maintain his high level of energy, Roosevelt needed to boost his health with daily protein and nourishment. As an avid hunter, he shot wild game. His wild game was cooked and served on a platter fit for a president. Steak with gravy was a favorite dish. In order to enjoy the tasty game over the course of several days, however, he needed to prevent the meat from spoiling. Preserving a hundred pounds of meat required four quarts of rock salt combined with four pounds of brown sugar [5]. The meat would have to be layered between the salt-and-sugar mixture, then covered in brine [5]. By this tried-and-true summertime method, frontiersmen like Roosevelt could preserve meat for weeks, even months. In the winter, carcasses of wild game could be hung outside to freeze.

Plenty of unspoiled, edible meat meant that this passionate outdoorsman could eat like a nobleman. And he certainly did. Not only did Roosevelt have a taste for wild game, but he savored comfort foods that came with a sizable pairing of appetizing meat. He could devour an entire chicken in one sitting [6]. His fried chicken could only be relished when it was soaked in a generous helping of white gravy. And the White House received many gifts of wild game to please the president's adventurous taste buds [6].

Had Roosevelt had access to a modern convenience—the freezer—to store wild game after every successful hunting trip, he'd have labored less to preserve the meat. No single man, no matter how huge his carnivorous appetite, could ever finish off the entirety of meat after a large kill. The freezer would've been exceptionally handy.

The carcasses of the wild animals Roosevelt hunted would've been packaged in the correct portions, to be lifted out of the freezer and cooked to serve a precise number of people without letting any of the tender meat go to waste. Upon packaging his meat for the freezer, Roosevelt needed to minimize exposure to air. This could've been accomplished using vacuum-sealed bags or freezer paper. Meat that had been subject to freezer burn would've tasted terrible.

Plus, it helped that the wild game Roosevelt hunted was lean. Fatty carcasses tended to undergo freezer burn at a higher rate [7]. In any case, all the president had to do was portion his meat; three pounds per package would've suited his large family just fine. Then, he'd have to double-wrap his fresh meat and pop it into the freezer. Finally, Roosevelt needed to label the packages with the day's date, the specific cuts of meat, and how he'd like his cooks to prepare the meal, whether as steaks or strips.

And voila! Roosevelt would've avoided all the hassle in preserving meat using the old-fashioned tactic of rubbing in salt and topping with brine. An especially large freezer, such as one with dimensions of seventeen cubic feet, would've served his meat consumption needs superbly.

But freezers weren't invented until 1940—twenty-nine years after Roosevelt's second term as president. What a convenience a home freezer would've been to this lifelong hunter and carnivore. Despite earning a place among the great US presidents carved into

Mount Rushmore, Roosevelt didn't live long enough to see the invention of the home freezer. The naturalist and accomplished US president died on January 6, 1919—not from a hunting-related injury, but from a blood clot lodged in his robust heart.

39

SACAGAWEA AND THE POCKET TRANSLATOR

Language barriers have continually existed since the dawn of the world's first civilizations, whether between Neanderthals and early humans or the later Greeks and the Egyptians. It was no different in 1804, during the Lewis and Clark expedition in the United States.

Captain Meriwether Lewis was tasked with exploring the length and breadth of the Missouri River. The United States had just purchased Louisiana from Napoleon for twenty-seven million dollars [1]. The 828,000 square miles of virgin land invited exploration, and President Thomas Jefferson made plans to do so [1]. He delegated the role to Lewis, who chose Lieutenant William Clark to co-lead the westward expedition [1].

A team of fifty men formed the Corps of Discovery. They pushed their boat up the Missouri River. Lewis and Clark observed the land, particularly noting new plant species, native animals, soil types, and the unique climate of the explored areas [1]. Lewis recorded his discoveries, some of which included the Douglas fir, the ponderosa pine, the grizzly bear, and the prairie dog [1].

Diplomacy with the Native Americans was also on Jefferson's agenda. Tribes traded with expedition members and offered food, guides, and entertainment to sweeten their journey [1]. The exploration up the Missouri River continued, but with the addition of two new individuals who served as interpreters: the French-Canadian Toussaint Charbonneau and a young Shoshone woman named Sacagawea.

Charbonneau spoke French and, having spent significant time with Native Americans, a tribal language called Hidatsa. Sacagawea, who became one of his two wives, was fluent in her native Shoshone and Hidatsa [2]. Lewis and Clark, as well as most of the corps members, spoke English—but one member was also conversant in French [2]. Together, this band of explorers could communicate successfully amongst each other, and with the natives they encountered during their expedition.

Sacagawea was barely seventeen when in 1805 she gave birth to her and Charbonneau's son, Jean Baptiste. Two months later, Sacagawea, carrying her baby in a cloth bag secured on her back, set forth with the explorers to fulfill their duties of exploring the Louisiana Purchase, and to possibly confirm the location of the legendary Northwest Passage.

They needed horses to reach the Pacific, and to transport supplies over the rugged terrain of the Rocky Mountains. The Shoshone kept a herd of horses that Lewis and Clark knew they could purchase once they reached the edge of the Rockies after traveling up-river [2]. Sacagawea's language skills would be useful in the negotiations.

As an interpreter for Lewis and Clark, Sacagawea's abilities went beyond helping the expedition navigate intimidating and unchartered mountain passes. She also identified roots and berries that could be safely eaten, as well as plants and herbs that held medicinal properties [3].

The young Sacagawea led Lewis and Clark's expedition to the Pacific—their intended destination—and back. It was 1806, and the corps had miraculously averted near-fatalities from the barrage of flash floods, illnesses, and shortages of food that had threatened them with little remorse.

Throughout the two-year expedition, the resourceful Sacagawea was recognized as a gifted translator. Since she could speak Hidatsa, her words were understood by her husband, Charbonneau. And Charbonneau, also speaking French, communicated with the French-speaking corps member, who in turn translated the information to English for Lewis and Clark. A whirlwind of languages, effectively translated, made the expedition a notable success.

Now, had Sacagawea only had access to a modern convenience—the pocket translator—any chance of misinformation would have been thwarted. It took a great deal of luck and confidence for the expedition to avoid being accidentally misled by potentially erroneous interpretations. Danger could have befallen any one of them, as it nearly did, by running into hostile tribes who misunderstood words or intentions. Illness could have also stolen the lives of corps members who inadvertently consumed inedible plants when mishearing that a berry was tasty rather than toxic. A highly reliable alternate strategy would have been to use a pocket translator, had it been available in the eighteenth and nineteenth centuries. Lewis or Clark would have simply had to speak into the device, which would've instantly translated their spoken English into Hidatsa, allowing Sacagawea and Charbonneau to understand clearly and, with several aha-moments, confidently guide the corps in the most opportune direction.

It may be argued that, if Lewis and Clark utilized a pocket translator during their expedition, Sacagawea's interpretation services would've been unnecessary. This assumption is unmistakably wrong. Sacagawea served a dual purpose: the young mother with her infant sent an important message of peace and cooperation to the fierce, defensive natives the corps encountered on their trek. Simply, the Corps of Discovery seemed far friendlier when led by a gentle female carrying an innocent child [2]. Under dangerously unfamiliar conditions, it's unlikely a pocket translator could've single-handedly achieved such instant harmony between foreign groups of people who remained rightfully on guard.

Sacagawea would have valued the pocket translator even more so when it came to her son, Jean Baptiste. Lewis had a strong interest in educating the young boy, whom he nicknamed Pomp, and asked for permission to raise him. Parting from her child would've been emotionally wrenching. A pocket translator might've allowed Sacagawea to wholeheartedly understand Lewis' intention and perhaps feel less saddened by leaving her six-year-old behind in St. Louis. It would've been preferable to hear such a sensitive proposal straight from the horse's mouth, or, in this case, the pocket translator. Otherwise, the result would've resembled a game of telephone, where a sentence becomes warped as it spreads to multiple individuals. Nevertheless, Sacagawea's true feelings about the separation from her son remained unknown, but perhaps she felt heartened to start her new fur-trading expedition with her husband.

Unlike the old, wild unexplored west, people today have less to fear. The pocket translator, initially introduced as a machine translator in the mid-1950s then perfected over the decades, is essential for acquainting unfamiliar faces and starting friendly conversations, whether that be a Frenchman in China trying to buy a loaf of bread or a Bulgarian in Mongolia trying to rent a horse. The pocket translator is a modern convenience that deserves appreciation for bringing different societies together in sociable dialogue.

40

KING GEORGE VI AND AI VOICE GENERATOR

As the royal standby, Prince Albert never expected he'd be crowned king of the United Kingdom shortly after his brother, King Edward VIII, ascended to the throne. But his charming elder brother was haplessly smitten with an American divorcee named Wallis Simpson, and their whirlwind romance persuaded him to abdicate in 1936, after less than one brief year as king.

And so it was that Prince Albert became king in 1936. He took the name King George VI, and his adoring wife, Elizabeth Angela Marguerite Bowes-Lyon, stood faithfully by his side as queen. King George VI, however, was no ordinary royal: he endured a lifelong stutter.

His unusual predicament was worsened by the fact that his role as king obliged him to speak frequently before crowds who could tear him down with incessant mockery if they chose. He'd participated futilely in speech programs before [1]. Not only was King George VI distraught, but his close trusted circle was equally concerned. Devastated by his inability to express himself as eloquently as he would have liked in public, King George VI consulted a speech therapist. Lionel Logue was an Australian speech therapist who recommended crooning words loudly through an open window, practicing daily breathing exercises, and gargling with warm water

[1]. Lionel's methods focused on the physical aspects of the vocal apparatus, and he convinced the king that he did not suffer from a psychological flaw [1].

King George VI noticed improvements in his stutter after numerous ongoing therapy sessions. The king's public speech on May 5, 1938, took place in Glasgow, Scotland, before an eager, well-dressed crowd at the opening of the Empire Exhibition. Standing on a superbly decorated balcony and exuding a natural air of dignity, the king fared noticeably well in his speech, while taking intermittent pauses [2].

World War II broke out on September 1, 1939. Two days later, King George VI gave a moving speech, one that inspired the British people to sustain hope in the face of bleak days ahead. In a remarkable show of loyalty to his people, he decided to remain in the United Kingdom during the war instead of escaping with his family to the safety of Canada [3]. Once the war ended on September 2, 1945, the king was tasked with giving his Victory Day speech from his royal desk. This address, too, was presented with the poise and experience of a king who'd participated in regular radio broadcasts and public appearances over the years.

Throughout his reign, King George VI won great admiration from British citizens. The war was at the forefront of their minds, accompanied by the pains of hunger and the misery of inescapable poverty. But the British people held only deep respect for their king, who served to continually inspire them across the darkness of their war-torn days. Such love and reverence for the king was uncommon, as King George IV (Queen Victoria's uncle) was shamelessly ridiculed for his famous obesity. Rather, King George VI, made ordinary by his stutter and subsequent insecurity, was adored by the entire nation.

A great-grandson of the illustrious Queen Victoria, King George VI showed profound courage in striving to overcome his stutter, and in facing the British public with his disability. The king's despair in his ongoing struggle failed to hold him back from performing his royal duties—a sense of duty that he passed down to his eldest daughter, Elizabeth, who would later become one of the United Kingdom's most beloved queens.

Now, had King George VI only had access to a modern convenience—an AI voice generator—he'd have enjoyed a much easier, but possibly forgettable, reign. The artificial intelligence in text-to-speech assistive technology would have translated the king's written speeches into audible speech—along with the aristocratic Received Pronunciation accent for which the royal family was famously known. By uploading an audio sample of the king's authentic voice, then typing in the entirety of his royal speech, the AI system would have read the words aloud fluently, loosening the tight grip of self-consciousness and self-doubt on the reluctant king.

Had the AI voice generator converted his written words to eloquent speech, King George VI's radio broadcasts would've been like taking afternoon tea with cucumber sandwiches. No more worries about stuttering for the Windsor monarch. The system's natural language processing would have generated flowing speech very much in line with the expectations of the British public [3]. The technology's capabilities extended further, allowing control of voice tempo, volume, and pronunciation. An AI voice generator, had it been available in 1936, could have convincingly delivered the king's speeches in his regal baritone voice, saving him from the worry of stammering and stuttering during his spoken addresses to the public.

But the versatile artificial intelligence systems that effectively simulate a person's voice weren't released until early 2023—a good seventy years after King George VI. Indeed, this technology could have helped the king feel more confident in addressing his subjects. But because this modern convenience wasn't available at the time of King George VI, the gentle Windsor monarch—who, despite his struggles, persisted throughout his sixteen-year reign to live up to public expectations—is remembered today for his uncommon courage and for never accepting personal defeat.

41

FOLK MUSICIAN ELIZABETH COTTEN AND MUSIC STREAMING

The alluvial roots of American folk music run deep. The English, Irish, and Scottish sung treasure-troves of hundred-year-old folk music in their home pastures, and brought these pastoral tunes with them as they immigrated to America in the nineteenth century. During a span of forty years, from 1820 to 1860, waves of Irish immigrants entered the US through the port cities New York City, Boston, and Philadelphia [1]. Near the end of the century, more immigrants—and the music that eased their long ocean passages—poured through New York's Ellis Island.

European immigrants sung ballads of love and loss, honor, and betrayal on the ships' docks in the New World [2]. As ships departed and docked, taverns dotting the coast lit up with merry, intoxicated crowds crooning folk songs. Over multiple generations, songs marked by eternal themes of the heart passed by word-of-mouth [2].

During the Colonial era in the United States, the words to the early folk ballad "Barbara Allen" fell from the lips of a young Abraham Lincoln as he chopped wood in the wilderness of his Indiana home [2]. The music of Appalachia was inspired by hymns and fiddle music from the British Isles. In the American South, enslaved

Africans harvesting the fields audibly soothed the pain of hard physical labor by singing soulful tunes. And French settlers created Cajun music.

In later decades, cowboys in the West and Southwest sung their own versions of stirring ballads. References to the Old West infused their music, their songs illustrating the wild, picturesque life of working cowboys [2]. After taking a bullet to the chest, a dying cowboy dressed in white uttered his last words—words put to haunting lyrical melody in the folk song, "Streets of Laredo," believed to have been an American transplant of the old Irish song, "The Unfortunate Rake" [2].

Caught in the struggles and emotional hills and valleys of daily life, Americans developed their own folk music. Along with Appalachian music and cowboy songs came a slew of railroad songs, protest songs, and sea shanties [3]. Folk musicians noodled banjos and guitars, played the fiddle and double bass, and beat percussion instruments. America's rich musical harmonies varied from the eastern coast to the southern coast. Sea shanties in Massachusetts sounded recognizably different from Virginia bluegrass [3]. Despite the variations, one principle in folk music remained true: the music held greater importance than the musician.

This ideal is certainly true in the life of Elizabeth Cotten, who plucked the strings of her guitar upside down to create a repertoire of unforgettable folk music that continues to win over American hearts to this day. Despite her ordinary beginnings, the authenticity of her music echoed far louder, stronger, and more eloquently than anything else in the span of her unpretentious life.

Elizabeth Cotten, born in 1893 in Chapel Hill, North Carolina, was the daughter of a miner and a house cleaner. The left-handed youth dabbled on her brother's guitar while he was away at work. As a right-handed guitarist, he suggested she play the guitar the right way and admitted he was unable to teach her [8]. Practicing day and night, she taught herself to play melody with her thumb and the low notes with her two fingers [5].

A determined preteen, she went door to door, asking for work cutting vegetables or washing dishes [8]. Eventually, a lady hired her for seventy-five cents a month. Cotten earned enough to purchase her first Stella guitar [8]. The $3.75 price tag was as good as gold to the youth who'd spent three months working to pay it [5]. A young prodigy, Cotten learned a song by listening to it merely once, or, at most, twice.

At twelve years old, Cotten composed her timeless and most famous song, "Freight Train," a folk tune that, on the surface, was about the trains speeding past her home, but subtly expressed the longing for escape from the relentless prejudice toward African American children in the South [6]. Reluctantly, fifteen-year-old Cotten stopped the blues after being baptized and taught that she couldn't, as she said, "serve god and the devil at the same time" [8]. She became a teen bride and moved north to Washington, DC.

It was in the 1940s that Cotten was discovered for her precocious musical abilities. While she worked at a department store in the nation's capital, Ruth Crawford Seeger, matriarch of a famous American musical family, walked into the store with her daughters, one of whom got lost amid the clutter of holiday merchandise. The patient Cotten returned the crying child to her mother. Moved by Cotten's gentle demeanor, Seeger struck up a friendship with her. Seeger offered Cotten a job of cooking and looking after her children in her Maryland home [6].

164

The Seegers filled every corner of their affluent house with music. It was here that Cotten resumed her musicianship, playing the family guitar while tending to the needs of the family. Her inborn musical talent for the blues reemerged from its five-decades-long absence, and, with encouragement from the Seeger family, Cotten started giving public performances all across the country, where congressmen, like John F. Kennedy, sat mesmerized in the audience [4].

When the grown-up Seeger daughter played Cotten's poignant folk song "Freight Train," it became a sensation in England and in coffee houses in China [5]. Cotten's composition was copyrighted by other folk singers who modified the arrangement in order to transform it into a distinct work [4]. Cotten, who wasn't aware of how to challenge the copyright system, didn't immediately earn the full royalties to which she was entitled [5].

Now, had a modern convenience—music streaming services—been around at the time of Elizabeth Cotten, she'd have received the widespread fanfare she was justly due. As a folk musician who exuded wisdom and grace through her heartfelt vocals and guitar melodies, Cotten would've taken every opportunity to connect directly with her fans. As an entertainer on stage, she had the natural ability to connect with audiences. Most importantly, she wouldn't have been compelled to wait until her sixties to be recognized for her gift.

Plus, if music streaming had been available in the mid-1900s, Cotten would've put her kind face to her poignant, honest music—and the unfair copyright issues wouldn't have had a chance to see the light of day. Instead of continuing to work as a housekeeper until she was eighty, Cotten would have enjoyed much sooner her fair share in the limelight, not to mention the accompanying wealth.

At long last, in her early nineties, Cotten won a Grammy for Best Folk Performance. In 2022, she was posthumously inducted into the Rock and Roll Hall of Fame. Though Cotten's musical artistry is relatively known today, the availability of music streaming services fifty years ago would have catapulted her to national stardom and helped her become a celebrated household name early on. Such was the moving power of her raw, unpolished vocals and masterful guitar strumming—a rare combination that drew legions of folk music audiences.

But music streaming services didn't emerge until the end of the twentieth century, over a decade after Elizabeth Cotten's musical heyday. Popular music streaming platforms have the unprecedented capability to not only humanize musicians, like Cotten, but also their fans [7]. The deep emotional connections established between a passionate artist and an equally dedicated audience today are unlike any other in the timeline of musical performance history. Undoubtedly, considering Cotten's enduring musical legacy, she'd have profoundly touched the delicate sensibilities of far more American folk music enthusiasts than her humble persona ever dreamed possible.

42

TAO PORCHON-LYNCH AND SMART YOGA MATS

Tao Porchon-Lynch knew the secret to a lengthy and joyous life, which, according to this yoga legend, originated from "the breath of life"—the breath harnessed through the practice of yoga [1]. She believed so wholeheartedly in yoga's ability to promote health, happiness, and world peace that she taught yoga until a week prior to her death in 2020, at the age of 101.

Growing up in India to a French father and an Indian mother, Porchon found herself enamored with yoga from the tender age of eight [2]. From afar, she watched a group of boys practicing yoga on the breezy Pondicherry beach in French India and instantly fell head over heels with the strange movements [2]. Her aunt scolded her, saying yoga was for boys [2]. Undeterred, Porchon declared that if boys could do yoga, she could too. And so began her life-long love affair with yoga.

As a dark-haired young woman with a sparkle in her eyes and a face loved by the camera, Porchon strutted confidently into the glamorous world of modeling and acting. Modeling took her across the world to cities, like Paris, the fashion capital [2]. Chanel praised her as one of its top models [3]. Her films included the remake of *The Thief of Baghdad*, where she passionately played the multi-armed golden idol [1]. She taught yoga to fellow actors, like Fred Astaire, in between film takes [3].

At age 49, Porchon-Lynch gave up her life on the silver screen and entered the mystical world of yoga [2]. She'd always practiced yoga since she was first introduced to it as a girl on the shorelines of India, but she now took up the practice full time. She studied with Indra Devi, the First Lady of Yoga, who had introduced Indian yoga to the West. Nine years later, Porchon-Lynch became one of the founders of the Yoga Teachers Association [2]. After founding the Westchester Institute of Yoga in 1982, she certified hundreds of yoga teachers [4].

Nearing the age of sixty, Porchon-Lynch didn't let age slow her down. Her remarkable zest for life revitalized her enthusiasm for teaching yoga until she surpassed her hundredth year. When she was ninety-three, she won the Guinness World Records title for the oldest yoga teacher in the world [4]. She gave seven weekly yoga classes in New York, inspiring her dedicated students with the keen insight and wisdom that flowed from the heart of a truly genuine master yogi.

Porchon-Lynch was an unbridled, joyous spirit, who shone on anyone who crossed her path. Not even age caught up with her. Sporting silvery hair and a face full of gentle wrinkles, she maintained her reputation for always wearing high heels [4]. She could be seen wearing them while dancing the fox trot, waltz, and jitterbug. Ballroom dancing became her passion at the age of eighty-seven, when she first took up the sport. Porchon-Lynch won over 750 first-place awards since she graced the floor with dashing dance partners less than three times her age [3]. Confident, spirited, and never without a smile on her face, Porchon-Lynch epitomized what it meant to live the best day of her life every single day.

Clearly, Porchon-Lynch was an emboldened spirit, made stronger by her lifelong practice of yoga. Three hip replacements didn't stop her from continuing to practice and teach yoga, or from inspiring her long-time students with her electrified presence and indomitable gusto for all life had to offer. When asked why her surgeries didn't slow her down, she replied without missing a beat,

"I'm the boss" [1]. Nothing was impossible for a dynamic yoga instructor who carried the "dance of life" within her [1].

Since 1967, she'd been responsible for shaping the hearts, minds, and bodies of hundreds of yoga practitioners. If only a modern convenience—the smart yoga mat—had been around since that groovy decade, Porchon-Lynch would've accelerated the rate of learning for yoga instructors whom she taught and certified. Learning basic yoga poses takes anywhere from four to eight weeks of regular practice. But with the help of the smart yoga mat, eager students could've become proficient sooner.

The smart yoga mat is designed to teach yoga, suggesting in real-time ways to correct posture or moves when sensing how the body is positioned [5]. The untiring AI instructor carefully gathers data about a student's body movements [5]. In the event that instructors, like Porchon-Lynch, were fully booked, or when students couldn't attend classes because of a hectic schedule, the smart yoga mat would've served as a dependable replacement. Busy students would've squeezed in at least a few minutes of morning yoga without losing the valuable ground they'd already gained.

With a smart yoga mat, no one has an excuse to not fit a session of yoga into their day. Built with sensor fabric and sensors, the mat offers personalized recommendations to enhance an aspiring yoga student's game [6]. The mat even provides motivation on those days when yoga is the last activity on the minds of weary students. But given the mood-boosting powers of yoga, who'd want to miss a session? Though the motivation delivered by a smart yoga mat pales in comparison to the life legacy left by Porchon-Lynch, it's better than having zero encouragement at all.

But the yoga mat was only introduced to the world around 2014—nearly fifty years after Porchon-Lynch became a full-time yoga instructor. It was almost indisputable that earlier yoga students would've embraced this technology. The mat is a game-changer for practitioners whose busy schedules demand more time than they can give to the essential, life-enhancing practice of yoga. Porchon-Lynch would've loved that practitioners of all levels today have the opportunity to reawaken their enthusiasm for yoga and achieve their goals with the help of this modern convenience.

43

SIGMUND FREUD AND SMART SOFAS

Born in humble circumstances to a Jewish wool merchant and his wife in the Austro-Hungarian Empire in 1856, Sigmund Freud was an unremarkable young boy. But he was driven by ambitious dreams, loving the grandeur of fame even before he ultimately found it.

He invested himself in medical school studies at the University of Vienna. Upon graduating with a medical degree at the age of twenty-five, Freud began his career as a neurologist. In due course, he developed theories of the human psyche. During his work in Paris with Jean-Martin Charcot in 1885, he was introduced to the concept that hysteria originated in the mind and not the brain [1]. Hypnosis was a known treatment of the era for patients labeled as hysterics, and, having witnessed Charcot hypnotizing those who sought medical care, Freud began the practice of hypnotism on his own patients. For a decade, he committed to using hypnosis to relieve symptoms of hysteria.

Upon Freud's return to Vienna, he began a partnership with another physician named Josef Breuer. One of Breuer's patients, a young woman addressed in medical literature as Anna O., complained of suffering from hysterics [2]. Rather than treat her with conventional hypnosis, Breuer encouraged her to express her symptoms freely [2]. To Breuer's surprise, venting her feelings alleviated her symptoms, at least for the short-term, which he attributed to the cathartic release of the pent-up emotions that drove her into uncontrolled fits of mental anguish [3].

After Breuer's discovery, Freud reviewed medical cases from a century earlier and analyzed symptoms of hysteria in his own patients—fundamental research that led to him developing a technique known as free association. The Austrian neurologist put his theories in writing in *Studies in Hysteria*, a publication he co-authored with Breuer [4]. For Freud, it was in the seat of the unconscious mind where the secrets to mental health could be unlocked.

Freud believed a battle between the conscious mind and the unconscious mind took place in patients afflicted with hysteria [3]. But by uninhibitedly expressing random thoughts as rapidly as they entered the conscious mind, the hidden warriors fighting stealthily in the unconscious mind could be subdued. Hysteria symptoms, from abrupt silences to incomprehensible stuttering, were symbols of unearthed conflicts. But free association—which helped bring besieging troubles within the unconscious to the surface—freed patients from the unseen aggressors wreaking havoc in their minds.

Eventually discarding hypnosis, Freud focused on the concept of free association [5]. The neurologist soon developed psychoanalysis, a term he coined in 1896. A psychological specialty, psychoanalysis involved the restructuring of components in emotional reasoning [6]. In order to perform psychoanalysis, Freud needed to encourage his patients to feel comfortable enough to open up. He increased his patients' ease by asking them to recline on a sofa. Once comfortable, they openly discussed nuisances, complaints, or positive life experiences—any topic on heaven or earth they might entertain. Hastily, the neurologist wrote down his patients' revelations, then analyzed the notes.

Since a feeling of ease preceded free expression, it was critical to Freud's practice that his patients relaxed on appropriate furniture. Nineteenth-century patients in Freud's office laid down on an upholstered sofa with rolled arms that formed an all-around rolling curve. Whether leather or fabric, the sofa was plump enough to promote an acceptable level of relaxation, allowing Freud to make headway with his psychoanalysis.

But an upholstered Chesterfield sofa was a rudimentary style of furniture compared to today's assortment of luxurious sofas. A smart sofa—a modern convenience that remains the epitome of comfort—would have delivered far greater ease to every one of Freud's patients. When complaining of symptoms of hysteria or other mental malaise, they'd have been instructed to lie down on the smart sofa, manipulate its high-tech features to relax to the max, express a continuous stream of their innermost thoughts, and experience relief from their mental health issues.

A smart sofa delivered what no sofa before it ever did. Firstly, a smart sofa, also known as a tech sofa, would've attracted patients with its sleek, contemporary design. Freud's patients would've been drawn to the elongated curvature, felt compelled to plop down, and relaxed on the large headrests to prepare for their session. Touch-control LED lights built into the smart sofa would have literally brightened up their hour-long session, especially for those simultaneously suffering from seasonal-affective disorder. Undoubtedly, Freud would've seen that his patients were sufficiently hydrated by filling the stainless-steel cups in the smart sofa with sparkling water, juice, or whatever non-alcoholic beverages his patients preferred. Bluetooth speakers built into the smart sofa would have released soothing classical music, further lulling Freud's patients into productive states of deep relaxation. Surrounding the cup holders would have been a series of controls, such as those capable of shifting the headrest and others switching on the heat. Heated seats would have tripled his patients' physical well-being and, thereby, his success with the hour of therapy. Those patients insisting on maximum comfort to ensure an optimal session would have made good practical use of the smart sofa's power reclining capabilities.

Now, if only Freud had access to a smart sofa in the nineteenth century, he'd have had reason to boast of infinitely more patient successes. After all, who might've resisted talking freely while sprawled out on the comfy seat of a smart sofa? Indeed, the father of psychoanalysis would've had little trouble transporting his patients into states of profound relaxation, inspiring them to effortlessly release trapped internal thoughts, and healing even the most deep-rooted cases of hysteria. But tech sofas weren't introduced until the twenty-first century, over a hundred years after Freud revolutionized psychotherapy. Fortunately for today's patients, smart sofas make a therapist visit an event to anticipate.

44

QUEEN VICTORIA AND LANGUAGE LEARNING APPS

The Victorian Age sprang from the very name, Queen Victoria, a dignified woman of nimble mind mixed with tastes particular to the common folks over whom she ruled. She was a fan of English novelist Charles Dickens, like all levels of social classes, and immersed herself in the moving stories of an author whose books never went out of print. Being an avid reader, a keen listener, and a speaker with a silvery voice, Queen Victoria entertained an affinity for languages.

Speaking fluent English, she communicated daily with members of her royal court. As the daughter of a mother of German descent, Queen Victoria spoke German growing up in the palace. Soon after she ascended the throne, the queen proposed to her dashing third cousin, German-born Prince Albert of Saxe-Coburg and Gotha, and the married couple discussed important matters of state in German, even sharing jokes in the West Germanic language. The passionate lovebirds could also be heard arguing in her husband's native tongue [1]. Queen Victoria, a happily married romantic, rolled off her tongue words in French and Italian. The queen even studied Latin and dabbled in Urdu and Hindi, which, at the time, were known as Hindustani, the language of India. She served, after all, as empress of India from 1876 until she died in 1901.

Queen Victoria's family tree stretched extensively, growing branches that reached far and wide. Though she detested babies, she gave birth to nine, many of whom later became monarchs in Europe, from the crown prince of Prussia to the grand duchess of Hesse and the prince of Wales [2]. Hence, the queen was related to a significant number of royals in Europe. In order to communicate with her family members, she needed exemplary language skills. Furthermore, Queen Victoria dined with foreign monarchs in her grand palace and visited others in their lavish kingdoms [2]. So to earn proper respect and show courtesy to her royal peers, the queen made it a point to be multilingual. After all, Queen Victoria presided over a magnificent, far-reaching empire, where the golden sun never set. It was in her best interests to know the cultures and languages of her subjects around the world.

But one peculiarity irked members of her royal court more than anything else: her friendship with the Indian-born Abdul Karim [3]. His initial role was to teach her Urdu phrases so that she could greet the Indian princes invited to an extravagant banquet held at the time of her Golden Jubilee [3]. Karim himself was fluent in Urdu and Persian. The Indian clerk was hand-selected to assist the queen at her Golden Jubilee, and before departing for England, he picked up some rudimentary English [3].

Karim remained by the queen's side well after her celebration of fifty years on the throne. At her request, the twenty-four-year-old Indian taught the British sovereign phrases in Urdu. Queen Victoria intended to communicate directly with her Indian servants in the language then known as Hindustani—and to their astonishment, the British queen did just that.

One gloomy English afternoon, the queen's Indian tutor cooked chicken curry and served it to her. Upon enjoying the spicy cuisine with unprecedented royal delight, the queen added the exotic dish to her regular schedule of meals [3]. Queen Victoria further indulged herself in the intricacies of exotic Indian culture, intensifying Karim's lessons in English so they could exchange words without going through intermediaries [3]. She began writing to him in her native tongue. Her letters revealed the extent of their close, platonic friendship—a thorn in the sides of her royal courtiers. But their biases did not deter the queen, who continued to shower Karim with extraordinary luxuries, perks, and gifts [3].

Now, had Queen Victoria only had access to a modern convenience—the language learning app—she'd have picked up Urdu within a matter of months and satisfyingly annoyed her flummoxed courtiers even further. "Yes, haan, I'd like more curry," she'd answer with a nod, when asked by her Indian servants whether she'd like a second helping. "It's quite acha, quite good, this curry," she'd remark, after putting a heaping spoonful into her mouth. It didn't take long for a language learning app to teach an eager student to say "yes" or "good" in Urdu. And the app would've delivered the correct pronunciation, accents and all, making the language learning experience authentic and enriching.

Given the speed at which an individual with an agile mind and determination could master a foreign language, Queen Victoria, as empress of India, would've soon been able to directly address the entire Urdu-speaking populace in their native language. It wouldn't have been a surprise if she gave an hour-long speech in Urdu after remaining studiously engrossed in her language learning app. The ability to instantly connect and win the esteem of her subjects by communicating in a mutually shared language would have led to uproarious applause and long-standing respect for the British monarchy.

Not only would Queen Victoria have been able to speak fluent Urdu and Hindi, she'd have quickly learned to write in those languages as well. The intelligent queen did in fact fill several journals in Urdu and Hindi [1]. Nor would Karim have been left out with the introduction of language learning apps, as he'd have picked up English from A to Z far sooner, even learning to stress his words with the aristocratic Received Pronunciation British accent. The queen, being a night owl, and her most valued Indian assistant, would have chatted long after sunset, switching from English to Urdu and back again as it suited their fancies. During their deep and lengthy conversations, they would've consulted the reliable language learning app for translations of any unusual or sophisticated words, ensuring only brief interruptions. And these two close friends would have gossiped freely in Urdu, scorning the jealousy and bias shown by the queen's royal associates toward Karim—doing so even in their presence, without causally infuriating them further.

But language learning apps weren't available in the era of Queen Victoria, as they were released only as recently as 2011—over a century after the popular queen exhaled her last breath. Had this modern convenience been invented earlier, the Victorian Age would have been infused with exotic flair, and, thanks to Karim, Indian curry would have stayed on the lunch menus of people everywhere the shining sun never set.

45

BUFFALO BILL'S PONY EXPRESS RIDES AND EMAIL

Extraordinary lore surrounded Wild West legend William Frederick Cody, better known as Buffalo Bill. He was a master showman, entertaining rough-and-tumble audiences with shots fired from his rifle (which he named Lucretia Borgia after the Italian femme fatale), daring horse rides with spitfire cowboys, and recreations of the buffalo hunts that gave him his world-famous moniker [1]. Buffalo Bill's successful career as one of America's principal Wild West entertainers spanned an impressive forty-five years [2].

But Buffalo Bill had another trick up the long sleeve of his raw hide coat. He'd served as a rider in the nation's express mail service, the Pony Express. Historians remain unable to fully verify his participation in delivering America's mail to the West. But Buffalo Bill did pen in his autobiography his brief stint as a rider, stacking more excitement onto the plate of his already-legendary persona [1].

Buffalo Bill was one of the most famous and celebrated riders for the Pony Express, a short-term operation that sent its first rider off on April 3, 1860. A year later and in financial ruin, the Pony Express coordinated its final delivery before ending on October 26, 1861. The installation of the transcontinental telegraph put an end to the Pony Express' eighteen-month heyday [3].

During the year-and-a-half that the Pony Express remained in full swing, riders on horseback sped from the east to the west coast, delivering bags of mail within ten days—the swiftest means of communication the east had with the newly added western state of California. Galloping by the shortest routes was faster than relying on stagecoaches bumbling along at the speed of tropical sloths.

Pony Express riders showed no fear in braving the untamed Wild West. Their adventures began in Missouri and took them nearly 2,000 miles, first to Utah before finally reaching their destination in northern California [3]. Riders switched tired horses, chugged bottles of water, rested for a short spell, and dropped off their twenty-pound bags of mail in the stations built along the route.

What a treacherous route it was, taking riders through flattened terrains and steep mountainsides. They pushed onward, even when moonlight provided the only guidance [4]. Riders galloping seventy-five miles each day faced blinding blizzards and parching heat. Despite harsh weather conditions and rough terrain, their precious mail pouches were considered more important than the lives of the riders and their horses [3]. Riders faced threats from hostile Native American tribes. Stations were raided, horses were stolen, and defenseless station operators working in isolation were killed [3]. Dehydration along the trails was possible, as well as being savagely bitten by swarms of insects.

It took a special rider to serve in the Pony Express for the generous monthly sum of $100. Three important criteria for riders included being small, lightweight, and Wild West tough [3]. Though eligible riders were small in stature, they gained a reputation that made them larger than life. It so happened that a young Buffalo Bill fit this description, applied, and was hired as a Pony Express rider.

Fifteen years old, Buffalo Bill started his short career with the Pony Express [3]. After working a span of a few months, he famously galloped on his horse from Red Butte Station in Wyoming until he reached Pacific Springs. He didn't stop there, but rode back, for a total of 300 miles within twenty-two consecutive hours [3]. Along the route, Buffalo Bill narrowly escaped Native American warfare and thieves—the likes of which only a buccaneer like Buffalo Bill could outsmart—and lived to tell the tale, if indeed they were embellished tales or authentic accounts.

The Wild West in the nineteenth century was truly wild, and mail service wasn't anywhere near as uneventful as it is today. Pony Express riders were willing to sacrifice their lives to be of service to the Americans who wanted their handwritten first-class letters delivered promptly.

Now, had Buffalo Bill and other Pony Express riders had access to a modern convenience—email—they wouldn't have had to risk life and limb to deliver messages by the fastest method known at the time. Rather than die from thirst, freeze to death, or be killed in ambush, Pony Express riders could've benefitted from a safer method of sending messages back and forth. Email, had it been around in 1860, would've made it far easier, quicker, and safer to communicate. No one sending email runs into warring native tribes or gallops seventy-five miles day and night to ensure a message is delivered. Instead of taking ten days for President James Buchanan's letter to reach California Governor John Downey, email would've been received instantly—and riders like Buffalo Bill wouldn't have had to risk everything [5].

Of course, utilizing email instead of the Pony Express would've erased some of the wild from the Wild West. How many audacious escapades would've resulted from sending email? Perhaps, instead of being ambushed by unreceptive Native American tribes, a sender or recipient of an email would have risked being attacked by vicious malware. However, the threat is hardly comparable. While the first Pony Express ride was met with bands playing and audiences enthusiastically singing, shouting, and waving flags from rooftops, email hardly received all the fanfare. At most, when receiving an email in its earliest days, recipients could hear a perky "You've got mail!" But unlike the Pony Express, that was the unimpressive extent of the celebration.

Plus, Buffalo Bill wouldn't have had to use up eight of his nine lives during his time as a rider with the Pony Express. While this might've been comforting to his family and friends, it would've left a gaping hole in the enduring lore of the American Wild West. If email had been around over a century ago, Buffalo Bill might not have made headlines for his 300-mile nonstop ride. But a colorful character like him would've found other ways to be celebrated, as he so famously did.

Buffalo Bill didn't need email, but presidents, like Abraham Lincoln, would've benefited from faster means of communication. Around the time of the Pony Express, the country was on the brink of the Civil War. Presidents, senators, governors, and other politicians needed to communicate with lightning-fast speed. Email would've delivered this service in a dignified, presidential manner—and no one would've waited several anxious days to hear the latest news, including the results of critical political elections.

But email was only invented in 1971—just over a hundred years after the Pony Express enterprise began and dissolved. Today, email senders and recipients enjoy exchanging messages without heightened risk to life and liberty. Certainly, if email had existed in 1860, Buffalo Bill wouldn't have seen the need to take such news-worthy risks as he did while employed by the Pony Express. But he still would've leveraged his many other versatile talents to express the true pioneering spirit of the American Wild West.

46

POLITICIANS AND
AI POLITICAL SPEECH WRITING TECHNOLOGY

Politicians have long given speeches to prove an argument, enlighten audiences, and stir their emotions, or, as Cicero succinctly declared, "docere, delectare, et movere" [1]. Cicero's own speeches, such as his "First Speech Against Catiline," delivered in the Roman Senate in 63 B.C.E., was empowering, but riddled with long-windedness and repetition—as political speeches are, by design.

Cicero's speech took deliberate aim at senator Catiline, who he alleged had plotted to overthrow the Roman Senate [2]. The famed orator sprinkled his attack with accusatory descriptors, from "disgraceful" to "licentious wickedness" and "corruption," all in reference to the behaviors of the maligned senator [3]. The verbose speech likely took Cicero a solid hour or more to orate, which was the average length of a typical political speech.

In some cases, political speeches could go on for quite some time. It wasn't unheard of for today's politicians to strive to make their point orally for twenty-four straight hours, tiring themselves and their audiences to the point of needing medical attention. These filibusters, a time-wasting tactic that demanded a remarkable level of verbal endurance, were intended to stall legislation.

While the seldom-occurring filibuster would send fellow congressmen into a daze, others relied on briefer speeches, such as floor speeches lasting five hours.

No matter how long a politician spoke, someone had to write the speech. Trusted aides were usually tasked with the laborious job of writing speeches, mostly because politicians knew little about the subjects firsthand [4]. If he gave erroneous statistics while reading his speech, well, he wasn't to blame—the speech writer was [4]. Thanks to speech writers, slick politicians were conveniently off the hook.

These trusted speech writers followed a specific pattern while writing political rhetoric. The core proposition would first be expressed, and memorable ones were always preferred. A noteworthy political speech included elements of storytelling, which required extra hours of research. The political aides reached out to the community to find constituent members impacted in some way by the core proposition and presented real, relatable people to audiences. Two supporting arguments plus evidence accompanied by a series of dreary statistics effectually rounded out the dramatic tale [5]. Of course, politics wouldn't be what it is without rebuttals. So the political speech writer would've included opponents' potential arguments and the manner in which the politician disagreed. The entire speech would be tidily wrapped up with ongoing repetition of all the above. And a speech of several hours long was concluded.

The most time-consuming part of the speech, aside from tirelessly orating it, was the research into the opposition, their weaknesses, and their past—especially one that could've been advantageously exploited [5]. Once the speech was written, it would've been read by the politician verbatim. His only objective was to stay on message, in order to escape attack and remain in office another day [4]. By traveling the safest route during his speech, the politician risked nothing—and gained nothing [4].

Long gone are the days when political speeches inspired citizens, emboldened them to pursue moral actions, or gave them the strength to pull through the nation's bleakest days. Knowledge and passion breathed life into the best political speeches—as Cicero proved during his heyday in the Roman Senate. These days, political speeches are no more than rambling narratives without purpose or passion. Now, to that end, almost anyone could write a political speech—including a modern convenience, AI.

Algorithms are capable of determining the structure and content of today's political speeches. AI would peruse thousands of political speeches stored in databases, then be trained to write speeches of its own [6]. With machine-learning, it would learn what to expect word after word from the beginning of the speech through the very end [6]. The AI would achieve grammatical correctness and smooth transitions [6]. Unsurprisingly, today's AI is inherently capable of writing the US president's State of the Union Address.

Much like all political speeches, this annual speech followed a predictable pattern [7]. The president would rattle off a list of accomplishments, throw out touching stories about a few lucky, or not-so-lucky, guests in attendance, soberly discuss the problems of the day, then finish off on a high note about the glorious times the nation was about to live through [7]. The power of AI systems was that they could converse like humans, thereby giving a president a surefire way to relate to audiences.

AI would've been an ideal vehicle for today's political speech writing environment, because the system is entirely devoid of emotion. It's unlikely that AI would inject passion into a speech, making the message less poignant, less memorable—and yet utterly safe for the politician's career. And isn't that what politicians want these days? A long, uneventful career? While not even the most advanced AI could ever replicate the eloquence of Abraham Lincoln's *Gettysburg Address* or the iconic message in the inaugural address given by John F. Kennedy or Ronald Reagan's inspirational *Berlin Wall* speech during the height of the Cold War, the system is reliable for everyday floor speeches routinely given by regular politicians.

But AI political speech writing technology only gained ground in 2016, when United States congressmen and even the Israeli president used it to draft speeches that wowed unsuspecting audiences. Plus, for once, everyday political speeches could be entertaining and worth hearing, especially when written by AI systems that scoured online media and databases to capture the essence of comedians. A speech could be punctuated with humor after AI grabbed punchlines from online sources, or offer a load of fun when mimicking the colloquialisms of legendary sports figures. Similarly, AI could be powerful when channeling the thought processes of historic civil rights leaders and revered authors. While AI political speech writing tools will never be capable of authentically inspiring a country during its toughest moments, it is certainly a modern convenience that's useful for the rigors of ordinary life.

CONCLUSION

Historical figures missed out on a diverse range of modern conveniences that would've remarkably enhanced their everyday comfort. But future conveniences will put today's society in the same boat as our uncomfortable predecessors. Upgrades to existing inventions and entirely new conveniences are constantly emerging, giving our comfortable lives an even greater dose of ease.

It's only a matter of time before the world will be under a deluge of a vaster assortment of modern conveniences, helping us live even more smartly, comfortably, and expediently. We might have an inkling of what's ahead over the next millennia. But for the most part, we will not quite know what we're missing—but those looking back on us certainly will.

Thank you for reading
Modern Conveniences That Would've Rewritten History.
If you enjoyed these snippets of world history, it'd mean a great deal if you could leave a review at your favorite retailer and help other history lovers discover amusing books.

Visit www.riyapresents.com

BIBLIOGRAPHY

1. Alexander the Great and Antibiotics

[1] Matthias, Meg. n.d. "How Did Alexander the Great Really Die?" Encyclopedia Britannica. https://www.britannica.com/story/how-did-alexander-the-great-really-die.

[2] "6.4 The Spread of Hellenistic Culture – Teaching California." n.d. Accessed February 10, 2023. https://www.teachingcalifornia.org/inquiry-sets/6-4-the-spread-of-hellenistic-culture/.

2. Prehistoric Natufian Bakers and Bread Machines

[1] Zeldovich, Lina. "14,000-Year-Old Piece Of Bread Rewrites The History Of Baking And Farming." NPR, July 24, 2018. https://www.npr.org/sections/thesalt/2018/07/24/631583427/14-000-year-old-piece-of-bread-rewrites-the-history-of-baking-and-farming.

[2] History.com. "The Prehistoric Ages in Order: How Humans Lived Before Written Records," October 21, 2019. https://www.history.com/news/prehistoric-ages-timeline.

[3] "NIHF Inductee Joseph Lee Made Bread History With His Invention," 2023. https://www.invent.org/inductees/joseph-lee.

3. Hippocrates and Electronic Medical Records

[1] Tsiompanou, E, and Spyros G. Marketos. 2013a. "Hippocrates: Timeless Still." Journal of the Royal Society of Medicine

106 (7): 288–92. https://www.ncbi.nlm.nih.gov/pmc/articles/PMC3704070/.

[2] Cunha, Burke A. 2004. "The Cause of the Plague of Athens: Plague, Typhoid, Typhus, Smallpox, or Measles?" Infectious Disease Clinics of North America 18 (1): 29–43. https://www.ncbi.nlm.nih.gov/pmc/articles/PMC7118959/.

[3] Laios, Konstantinos, Pavlos Lytsikas-Sarlis, Kostas Manes, M.-i. Kontaxaki, Marianna Karamanou, and George Androutsos. 2019. "Drugs for Mental Illnesses in Ancient Greek Medicine." Psychiatrik 30 (1): 58–65. https://pubmed.ncbi.nlm.nih.gov/31115355/.

[4] Honavar, Santosh G. 2020. "Electronic Medical Records – The Good, the Bad and the Ugly." Indian Journal of Ophthalmology, March. https://www.ncbi.nlm.nih.gov/pmc/articles/PMC7043175/.

4. Neanderthals and GPS

[1] Lorraine Boissoneault, "Neanderthals Hunted in Groups, One More Strike Against the Dumb Brute Myth," Smithsonian Magazine, June 27, 2018, https://www.smithsonianmag.com/science-nature/neanderthals-hunted-groups-one-more-strike-against-dumb-brute-myth-180969472/.

5. Nefertiti's Subjects and Stick Deodorant

[1] History.com. "Nefertiti - Queen, Bust & Husband Akhenaten," June 7, 2019. https://www.history.com/topics/ancient-egypt/nefertiti.

[2] Tyldesley, Joyce. "Nefertiti | Biography, Reign, Death, Tomb, Meaning, & Facts." Encyclopedia Britannica, July 20, 1998. https://www.britannica.com/biography/Nefertiti.

[3] "LibGuides: 8 Mythology: Clothes and Climate," n.d. Accessed February 11, 2023. https://arc.servite.wa.edu.au/mythology/egypt.

[4] Wu, Katherine J. "Ancient Egyptian Head Cones Were Real, Grave Excavations Suggest." Smithsonian Magazine, De-

cember 11, 2019. https://www.smithsonianmag.com/smart-news/ancient-egyptian-head-cones-were-real-grave-excavations-suggest-180973750/.

[5] St Fleur, Nicholas. "Head Cones in Ancient Egyptian Graves Cap Archaeological Debate." The New York Times, December 11, 2019. https://www.nytimes.com/2019/12/11/science/head-cones-ancient-egypt.html.

[6] Wikipedia contributors. "Deodorant." Wikipedia, March 31, 2023. https://en.wikipedia.org/wiki/Deodorant.

6. Stonehenge Builders and Construction Robots

[1] History.com. "Solving the Riddle of Stonehenge's Construction," February 19, 2020. https://www.history.com/news/solving-the-riddle-of-stonehenges-construction.

[2] History.com. "Stonehenge," February 3, 2020. https://www.history.com/topics/british-history/stonehenge.

[3] Geggel, Laura. "New Stonehenge Mystery: Who Were These 10 'Outsiders' Buried at the Site?" Livescience.Com, August 2, 2018. https://www.livescience.com/63240-cremation-burials-stonehenge.html.

7. Hammurabi and Smart Toothbrushes

[1] History.com. "What Was Life Like in Ancient Babylon?," July 21, 2022. https://www.history.com/news/daily-life-ancient-babylon-mesopotamia.

[2] ushistory.org. "Hammurabi's Code: An Eye for an Eye [Ushistory.Org]," n.d. https://www.ushistory.org/civ/4c.asp.

[3] Colgate. "History Of Toothbrushes And Toothpastes." Colgate, April 6, 2022. https://www.colgate.com/en-us/oral-health/brushing-and-flossing/history-of-toothbrushes-and-toothpastes#.

[4] "Dates, Caries, and Early Tooth Loss during the Iron Age of Oman." PubMed, March 1, 1999. https://doi.org/10.1002/(SICI)1096-8644(199903)108:3.

[5] PubMed. "Dentistry in Ancient Mesopotamia," n.d. Ac-

cessed February 20, 2023. https://pubmed.ncbi.nlm.nih.
gov/11324038/.

8. Ancient Egyptian Wives and Modern Paper

[1] "Marriage and Divorce in Ancient Egypt." n.d. Accessed
March 7, 2023. The Museum Journal. https://www.penn.museum/
sites/journal/1195/.

[2] Author. 2016. "Papyrus: A Brief History." May 23, 2016.
https://sites.dartmouth.edu/ancientbooks/2016/05/23/67/.

[3] Authors: Rebecca Capua. 1AD. "Papyrus-Making in Egypt."
The Met's Heilbrunn Timeline of Art History. January 1, 1AD.
https://www.metmuseum.org/toah/hd/pyma/hd_pyma.htm.

[4] "The History of Paper | American Forest and Paper Associa-
tion." n.d. https://www.afandpa.org/news/2021/history-paper.

[5] Britt, Kenneth W. 1999. "Papermaking | Process, History, &
Facts." Encyclopedia Britannica. July 26, 1999. https://www.britan-
nica.com/technology/papermaking.

[6] Hayes, Lee. 2018. "The Three P's: Papyrus, Parchment and
Paper." The University of Adelaide. May 2018. https://www.ade-
laide.edu.au/library/special/exhibitions/cover-to-cover/papyrus/.

9. The Great Library of Alexandria and eBooks

[1] "Library of Alexandria." n.d. Accessed February 19, 2023.
https://penelope.uchicago.edu/~grout/encyclopaedia_romana/
greece/paganism/library.html.

[2] "Library of Alexandria | Description, Facts, & Destruction."
2023. Encyclopedia Britannica. March 31, 2023. https://www.
britannica.com/topic/Library-of-Alexandria/The-fate-of-the-Li-
brary-of-Alexandria.

[3] Harlitz-Kern, Erika. 2019. "10 Facts About the Ancient
Library of Alexandria | Book Riot." BOOK RIOT. February 5, 2019.
https://bookriot.com/library-of-alexandria-facts/.

[4] UNESCO World Heritage Centre. n.d. "Alexandria, Ancient
Remains and the New Library - UNESCO World Heritage Centre."

https://whc.unesco.org/en/tentativelists/1822/.

10. King Henry VIII and Nutrition Apps

[1] Elton, Geoffrey R., and John S. Morrill. 2023. "Henry VIII | Biography, Wives, Religion, Death, & Facts." Encyclopedia Britannica. April 12, 2023. https://www.britannica.com/biography/Henry-VIII-king-of-England.

[2] McGreevy, Nora. 2020. "Researchers Find Remnants of Jousting Field Where Henry VIII Almost Died." Smithsonian Magazine, November 6, 2020. https://www.smithsonianmag.com/smart-news/jousting-henry-viii-tudor-history-180976221/.

[3] Chandler, Gemma. 2020. "Henry VIII Facts for Kids | National Geographic Kids." National Geographic Kids. April 29, 2020. https://www.natgeokids.com/uk/discover/history/monarchy/henry-viii-facts/.

[4] "Tudor Food and Eating." n.d. Accessed February 14, 2023. Historic Royal Palaces. https://www.hrp.org.uk/hampton-court-palace/history-and-stories/tudor-food-and-eating/#gs.pj33rl.

11. Bubonic Plague Doctors and Healthcare Robots

[1] History.com. "Black Death - Causes, Symptoms & Impact | HISTORY," March 28, 2023. https://www.history.com/topics/middle-ages/black-death.

[2] History, All About, and Winston Black. "Plague Doctors: Separating Medical Myths from Facts." Livescience.Com, May 19, 2020. https://www.livescience.com/plague-doctors.html.

[3] Bogart, Nicole, and Nicole Bogart. "Why Did Plague Doctors Wear Beaked Masks?" Coronavirus, April 10, 2020. https://www.ctvnews.ca/health/coronavirus/a-history-of-pandemic-masks-why-doctors-wore-beaks-during-the-plague-1.4890564.

[4] Trends, Market. "Impact of AI and Robotics in the Healthcare Industry." Analytics Insight, March 25, 2022. https://www.analyticsinsight.net/impact-of-ai-and-robotics-in-the-health-

care-industry/.

[5] Johnson, Khari. "Hospital Robots Are Helping Combat a Wave of Nurse Burnout." WIRED, April 19, 2022. https://www.wired.com/story/moxi-hospital-robot-nurse-burnout-health-care/.

12. Periwig Wearers and Baking Soda

[1] Reilly, Lucas. 2023. "Why Did People Wear Powdered Wigs?" Mental Floss, April 4, 2023. https://www.mentalfloss.com/article/31056/why-did-people-wear-powdered-wigs.

[2] Schlup, Murielle. 2023. "The Power and Pomp of the Wig." Swiss National Museum - Swiss History Blog. March 20, 2023. https://blog.nationalmuseum.ch/en/2023/02/the-power-and-pomp-of-the-wig/.

[3] Wikipedia contributors. "Sodium Bicarbonate." Wikipedia, April 17, 2023. https://en.wikipedia.org/wiki/Sodium_bicarbonate.

13. Ivan the Terrible and Power Recliners

[1] "Why Was Ivan so Terrible?" n.d. Accessed March 19, 2023. Sky HISTORY TV Channel. https://www.history.co.uk/articles/why-was-ivan-so-terrible.

[2] Andreyev, Nikolay. 2023. "Ivan the Terrible | Biography, Accomplishments, & Facts." Encyclopedia Britannica. March 14, 2023. https://www.britannica.com/biography/Ivan-the-Terrible.

[3] The Editors of Encyclopaedia Britannica. "Throne | Furniture." Encyclopedia Britannica, July 20, 1998. https://www.britannica.com/topic/throne.

14. Mozart and Joke-a-Day Apps

[1] Sadie, Stanley. "Wolfgang Amadeus Mozart | Biography, Music, The Magic Flute, & Facts." Encyclopedia Britannica, July 26, 1999. https://www.britannica.com/biography/Wolfgang-Amadeus-Mozart.

[2] Classic FM. "Mozart's Divertimento: A Musical Joke," n.d.

Accessed March 30, 2023. https://www.classicfm.com/composers/mozart/pictures/mozarts-15-birthday-facts/13/.

[3] Reilly, Lucas. "3 Dirty Songs by Mozart | Mental Floss." Mental Floss, February 26, 2014. https://www.mentalfloss.com/article/55247/3-dirty-songs-mozart.

[4] Wikipedia contributors. "Leck Mich Im Arsch." Wikipedia, January 13, 2023. https://en.wikipedia.org/wiki/Leck_mich_im_Arsch.

[5] Wikipedia contributors. "Bona Nox." Wikipedia, March 13, 2023. https://en.wikipedia.org/wiki/Bona_nox.

[6] Wikipedia contributors. "Difficile Lectu." Wikipedia, April 2, 2023. https://en.wikipedia.org/wiki/Difficile_lectu.

15. Vikings and Smart Showers

[1] "The History of the Viking Age." n.d. Accessed February 15, 2023. Sky HISTORY TV Channel. https://www.history.co.uk/shows/vikings/articles/the-history-of-the-viking-age.

[2] The Editors of Encyclopaedia Britannica. 2023. "Viking | History, Exploration, Facts, & Maps." Encyclopedia Britannica. March 28, 2023. https://www.britannica.com/topic/Viking-people.

[3] Dacey, James, and James Dacey. 2023. "Food Security Lessons from the Vikings." Eos, March. https://eos.org/articles/food-security-lessons-from-the-vikings.

[4] Christensen, Christian. 2021. "How Did Vikings Bathe? You Might Be Surprised." Scandinavia Facts (blog). October 11, 2021. https://scandinaviafacts.com/how-did-vikings-bathe/.

[5] Christensen, Christian. 2021a. "How Did Vikings Wash Their Hair and Brush Their Teeth?" Scandinavia Facts (blog). June 22, 2021. https://scandinaviafacts.com/how-did-vikings-wash-their-hair-and-brush-their-teeth/.

16. Rembrandt and the Selfie Stick

[1] "Rembrandt van Rijn, Self-Portrait, 1659," n.d. Accessed March 5, 2023. https://www.nga.gov/collection/highlights/rem-

brandt-self-portrait.html.

[2] "How Rembrandt Painted Self-Portraits," n.d. Accessed March 5, 2023. https://oldmasters.academy/old-masters-academy-art-lessons/how-rembrandt-painted-self-portraits.

[3] Life, Country, and Country Life. "In Focus: How Rembrandt's Self-Portraits Were Masterpieces of Art, Experimentation – and Even Marketing." Country Life, March 22, 2019. https://www.countrylife.co.uk/luxury/art-and-antiques/rembrandts-self-portraits-193977.

[4] Sotheby's. "Rembrandt's Self-Portrait and the Art of Reflection," July 7, 2020. https://www.sothebys.com/en/articles/rembrandts-self-portrait-and-the-art-of-reflection.

17. The Wei King's Physician Hua Tuo and Ibuprofen

[1] The MIT Press Reader. 2021. "A Hole in the Head: A Complete History of Trepanation." June 11, 2021. https://thereader.mitpress.mit.edu/hole-in-the-head-trepanation/.

[2] Learn, Joshua Rapp. 2016. "Drilling Deep: How Ancient Chinese Surgeons Opened Skulls and Minds." Smithsonian Magazine, December 5, 2016. https://www.smithsonianmag.com/science-nature/how-ancient-chinese-surgeons-opened-skulls-and-minds-180961286/.

[3] The Editors of Encyclopaedia Britannica. 2009. "Hua Tuo | Chinese Physician and Surgeon." Encyclopedia Britannica. May 8, 2009. https://www.britannica.com/biography/Hua-Tuo.

[4] Wikipedia contributors. 2023. "Cao Cao." Wikipedia, April. https://en.wikipedia.org/wiki/Cao_Cao.

[5] The Editors of Encyclopaedia Britannica. 1998. "Wei Dynasty | History & Culture." Encyclopedia Britannica. July 20, 1998. https://www.britannica.com/topic/Wei-dynasty.

[6] Halford, Gayle M, Marie Lordkipanidzé, and Steve P. Watson. 2012. "50th Anniversary of the Discovery of Ibuprofen: An Interview with Dr Stewart Adams." Platelets 23 (6): 415–22. https://pubmed.ncbi.nlm.nih.gov/22098129/.

[7] Derry, Sheena, Philip J Wiffen, Roger Moore, and Lars Bendtsen. 2015. "Ibuprofen for Acute Treatment of Episodic Tension-Type Headache in Adults." The Cochrane Library 2019 (5). https://www.ncbi.nlm.nih.gov/pmc/articles/PMC6457940/.

18. George Washington and Dental Implants

[1] George Washington's Mount Vernon. "False Teeth," n.d. Accessed February 27, 2023. https://www.mountvernon.org/library/digitalhistory/digital-encyclopedia/article/false-teeth/.

[2] National Archives. "President George Washington's First Inaugural Speech (1789)," August 30, 2022. https://www.archives.gov/milestone-documents/president-george-washingtons-first-inaugural-speech.

[3] Schultz, Colin. "George Washington Didn't Have Wooden Teeth—They Were Ivory." Smithsonian Magazine, November 7, 2014. https://www.smithsonianmag.com/smart-news/george-washington-didnt-have-wooden-teeth-they-were-ivory-180953273/.

19. Blackbeard and Electric Shavers

[1] Ullian, David M. "What Everyone Should Know About Blackbeard the Pirate." Amherst College. Accessed March 23, 2023. https://www.amherst.edu/users/U/dullian08/node/20554.

[2] The Editors of Encyclopaedia Britannica. "Pirates, Privateers, Corsairs, Buccaneers: What's the Difference?" Encyclopedia Britannica, n.d. https://www.britannica.com/story/pirates-privateers-corsairs-buccaneers-whats-the-difference.

[3] "Blackbeard (Aka Edward Teach) (U.S. National Park Service)," n.d. Accessed March 23, 2023. https://www.nps.gov/people/blackbeard.htm.

[4] Narula, Bhavna. "11 Astounding Facts About Pirate Hygiene You Never Heard Before." Medium, March 3, 2023. https://medium.com/lessons-from-history/11-astounding-facts-about-pirate-hygiene-you-never-heard-before-86fa9671f9fd.

20. Mona Lisa and Photo Metadata

[1] Zelazko, Alicja. "Why Is the Mona Lisa So Famous?" Encyclopedia Britannica, n.d. Accessed March 20, 2023. https://www.britannica.com/story/why-is-the-mona-lisa-so-famous.

[2] The Editors of Encyclopaedia Britannica. "Mona Lisa | Painting, Subject, History, Meaning, & Facts." Encyclopedia Britannica, November 26, 2008. https://www.britannica.com/topic/Mona-Lisa-painting.

21. Chichen Itza's Mayan Priests and Escalators

[1] "Pyramids in Latin America." 2019. History.Com. September 30, 2019. https://www.history.com/topics/ancient-americas/pyramids-in-latin-america.

[2] "Mayan Culture." n.d. Accessed March 10, 2023. https://www.cpskl2.org/cms/lib/MO01909752/Centricity/Domain/3479/mayan%20aztec%20cultures.pdf.

[3] Zelazko, Alicja. n.d. Accessed March 10, 2023. "What's Inside the Pyramid at Chichén Itzá?" Encyclopedia Britannica. https://www.britannica.com/story/whats-inside-the-pyramid-at-chichn-itz.

[4] The Editors of Encyclopaedia Britannica. 1998a. "Ah Kin | Mayan Religion." Encyclopedia Britannica. July 20, 1998. https://www.britannica.com/topic/Ah-Kin.

[5] "Maya Society - Hudson Museum - University of Maine." 2013. Hudson Museum. January 8, 2013. https://umaine.edu/hudsonmuseum/collections/william-p-palmer-iii/maya/maya-society/.

[6] Carpenter, Megan. 2019. "How the Escalator Forever Changed Our Sense of Space." Smithsonian Magazine, June 27, 2019. https://www.smithsonianmag.com/innovation/how-escalator-forever-changed-our-sense-space-180972468/.

22. Christopher Columbus and Over-the-Horizon Radar

[1] Morgan, Edmund S. 2009. "Columbus' Confusion About the New World." Smithsonian Magazine, October 1, 2009. https://

www.smithsonianmag.com/travel/columbus-confusion-about-the-new-world-140132422/.

[2] Flint, Valerie I.J. 1999. "Christopher Columbus | Biography, Nationality, Voyages, Ships, Route, & Facts." Encyclopedia Britannica. July 26, 1999. https://www.britannica.com/biography/Christopher-Columbus.

[3] "Christopher Columbus." n.d. Accessed April 3, 2023. Royal Museums Greenwich. https://www.rmg.co.uk/stories/topics/christopher-columbus.

[4] Dolce, Chris. 2016. "Interstate Traffic, Mayflies and 11 Other Weird Things That Have Shown Up on Radar." July 27, 2016. https://weather.com/science/news/radar-birds-bugs-bats-smoke-20130506.

[5] Wikipedia contributors. "Over-the-Horizon Radar." Wikipedia, April 14, 2023. https://en.wikipedia.org/wiki/Over-the-horizon_radar.

23. Ben Franklin and Smart Eyeglasses

[1] Cmccole. "Benjamin Franklin's Inventions | The Franklin Institute." The Franklin Institute, March 22, 2023. https://www.fi.edu/en/benjamin-franklin/inventions.

[2] Woodard, Amanda. "When Were Eyeglasses Invented and by Whom?" All About Vision, March 8, 2020. https://www.allaboutvision.com/eyeglasses/faq/invention-of-specs/.

[3] Jacewicz, Natalie. "What Did Nearsighted Humans Do Before Glasses?" NPR, July 7, 2016. https://www.npr.org/sections/health-shots/2016/07/07/484835077/what-did-nearsighted-humans-do-before-glasses.

[4] Gannon, Megan. "How Did Nearsighted People Manage Before Glasses Were Invented?" Livescience.Com, April 14, 2019. https://www.livescience.com/65229-nearsighted-people-before-glasses-invented.html.

[5] Hornberger, Theodore, and Gordon S. Wood. "Benjamin Franklin | Biography, Inventions, Books, American Revolution, &

Facts." Encyclopedia Britannica, April 13, 2023. https://www.britannica.com/biography/Benjamin-Franklin.

[6] "Benjamin Franklin, the Writer," n.d. Accessed March 15, 2023. https://www.americaslibrary.gov/aa/franklinb/aa_franklinb_writer_3.html.

[7] Ambiq. "Seeing the Future of Smart Glasses - Ambiq," October 18, 2022. https://ambiq.com/blog/seeing-the-future-of-smart-glasses/.

24. Inuit Igloos and Reversible Ceiling Fans

[1] "Igloo." n.d. Accessed February 21, 2023. The Canadian Encyclopedia. https://www.thecanadianencyclopedia.ca/en/article/igloo.

[2] "Inuit - Oil Lamp (Kudlik)." n.d. Accessed February 21, 2023. https://www.rct.uk/collection/95925/oil-lamp-kudlik.

[3] "The Healthy Journal - Gluten, Dairy, Sugar Free Recipes, Interviews and Health Articles." n.d. https://www.thehealthyjournal.com. https://www.thehealthyjournal.com/faq/can-you-have-a-fire-inside-an-igloo.

[4] Gadsby, Patricia. 2020. "The Inuit Paradox." Discover Magazine, July. https://www.discovermagazine.com/health/the-inuit-paradox.

[5] "Inuit." n.d. Accessed February 21, 2023. The Canadian Encyclopedia. https://www.thecanadianencyclopedia.ca/en/article/inuit.

[6] "NOVA | Arctic Passage | Igloo 101 (Answers) | PBS." n.d. Accessed February 21, 2023. https://www.pbs.org/wgbh/nova/arctic/iglo-answers.html.

25. Genghis Khan and the Paternity Test

[1] Bawden, Charles R. 2023. "Genghis Khan | Biography, Conquests, Achievements, & Facts." Encyclopedia Britannica. April 7, 2023. https://www.britannica.com/biography/Genghis-Khan.

[2] "Genghis Khan - Descendants, Empire & Facts." 2019. Histo-

ry.Com. June 6, 2019. https://www.history.com/topics/asian-histo-ry/genghis-khan.

[3] McLean, John. n.d. Accessed February 23, 2023. "Genghis Khan | World Civilization." https://courses.lumenlearning.com/suny-hccc-worldcivilization/chapter/genghis-khan/.

[4] Wikipedia contributors. 2023a. "The Secret History of the Mongol Queens." Wikipedia, January. https://en.wikipedia.org/wiki/The_Secret_History_of_the_Mongol_Queens.

[5] McKie, Robin. 2018. "We Owe It All to Superstud Genghis." The Guardian, February 14, 2018. https://www.theguardian.com/uk/2003/mar/02/science.research.

[6] Callaway, Ewen. 2015. "Genghis Khan's Genetic Legacy Has Competition." Nature, January. https://www.nature.com/articles/nature.2015.16767.

26. William Tell and the Modern Crossbow

[1] Wernick, Robert. 2004. "In Search of William Tell." Smith-sonian Magazine, August 1, 2004. https://www.smithsonianmag.com/history/in-search-of-william-tell-2198511/.

[2] "The Story of William Tell." n.d. Accessed April 6, 2023. https://arts.ms.gov/wp-content/uploads/2020/12/THE-STORY-OF-WILLIAM-TELL-Teacher-Copy.pdf.

[3] The Editors of Encyclopaedia Britannica. 2023a. "Crossbow | Definition, History, & Facts." Encyclopedia Britannica. March 10, 2023. https://www.britannica.com/technology/crossbow.

[4] Barber, Erik. 2020. "5 Archery Inventions That Changed the Game." Archery 360. September 8, 2020. https://archery360.com/2020/09/08/5-archery-inventions-that-changed-the-game/.

27. Montezuma II and the Chocolate Bar

[1] "History of Chocolate: Cocoa Beans & Xocolatl - HISTORY." 2022. History.Com. August 10, 2022. https://www.history.com/top-ics/ancient-americas/history-of-chocolate.

[2] Garthwaite, Josie. 2015. "What We Know About the Earliest

History of Chocolate." Smithsonian Magazine, February 12, 2015. https://www.smithsonianmag.com/history/archaeology-chocolate-180954243/.

[3] "The Legend of Montezuma's Lost Aztec Treasure." n.d. Accessed February 18, 2023. Sky HISTORY TV Channel. https://www.history.co.uk/articles/the-legend-of-montezuma-s-lost-aztec-treasure.

28. Galileo Galilei and the Event Horizon Telescope

[1] NASA Earth Observatory. n.d. Accessed March 3, 2023. "Planetary Motion: The History of an Idea That Launched the Scientific Revolution." https://earthobservatory.nasa.gov/features/OrbitsHistory.

[2] Cox, Lauren. 2021. "Who Invented the Telescope?" Space. Com, October. https://www.space.com/21950-who-invented-the-telescope.html.

[3] NASA Solar System Exploration. 2022. "Galileo's Observations of the Moon, Jupiter, Venus and the Sun," August 25, 2022. https://solarsystem.nasa.gov/news/307/galileos-observations-of-the-moon-jupiter-venus-and-the-sun/.

[4] "Galileo Is Accused of Heresy." 2022. History.Com. April 12, 2022. https://www.history.com/this-day-in-history/galileo-is-accused-of-heresy.

[5] "Working Together as a 'Virtual Telescope,' Observatories around the World Produce First Direct Images of a Black Hole." 2019. MIT News | Massachusetts Institute of Technology. April 10, 2019. https://news.mit.edu/2019/mit-haystack-first-image-black-hole-0410.

[6] "Telescopes Get Extraordinary View of Milky Way's Black Hole - Teachable Moments | NASA/JPL Edu." n.d. Accessed March 3, 2023. NASA/JPL Edu. https://www.jpl.nasa.gov/edu/news/2022/5/12/telescopes-get-extraordinary-view-of-milky-ways-black-hole/.

29. Raphael Sanzio and Digital Painting

[1] Culotta, Alexis. n.d. "The Role of the Workshop in Italian Renaissance Art." Khan Academy. Accessed March 26, 2023. https://www.khanacademy.org/humanities/renaissance-reformation/early-renaissancel/beginners-renaissance-florence/a/the-role-of-the-workshop-in-italian-renaissance-art.

[2] "Raphael | Biography, Artworks, Paintings, Accomplishments, Death, & Facts." 2023. Encyclopedia Britannica. April 2, 2023. https://www.britannica.com/biography/Raphael-Italian-painter-and-architect/Last-years-in-Rome.

[3] Stewart, Jessica. 2022. "8 Interesting Facts About Raphael, Master of the Italian Renaissance." My Modern Met, March. https://mymodernmet.com/raphael-sanzio-facts/.

[4] Wikipedia contributors. "Digital Painting." Wikipedia, April 19, 2023. https://en.wikipedia.org/wiki/Digital_painting.

[5] Stefyn, Nadia. 2022. "What Is Digital Painting? Your Guide to Getting Started | CG Spectrum." CG Spectrum News (blog). November 28, 2022. https://www.cgspectrum.com/blog/what-is-digital-painting.

30. Civil War Soldier James Winchell and Anesthesia

[1] Metwaly, Ahmed M., Mohammed M. Ghoneim, Ibrahim H. Eissa, Islam A. Elsehemy, Ahmad Mostafa, Mostafa M Hegazy, Wael M. Afifi, and Deqiang Dou. "Traditional Ancient Egyptian Medicine: A Review." Saudi Journal of Biological Sciences 28, no. 10 (June 19, 2021): 5823–32. https://www.ncbi.nlm.nih.gov/pmc/articles/PMC8459052/.

[2] Bryce, Emma. "How Did Doctors Perform Surgery before Modern Anesthesia?" Livescience.Com, February 21, 2022. https://www.livescience.com/surgery-before-anesthesia.

[3] Hollingham, Richard. "How Agonising Surgery Paved the Way for Anaesthetics." BBC Future, February 24, 2022. https://www.bbc.com/future/article/20200624-how-agonising-surgery-paved-the-way-for-anaesthetics.

[4] Shepard, Bob. "Anesthesia Came of Age during Civil War - Heersink School of Medicine News." UAB School of Medicine News, October 14, 2016. https://www.uab.edu/medicine/news/latest/item/282-he-s-pretty-spunky-anesthesia-comes-of-age-during-the-civil-war.

31. Mahatma Gandhi and Social Media

[1] "Gandhi's Persuasive Communication and Ideal Journalism | Relevance of Gandhi | Articles on and by Mahatma Gandhi," n.d. Accessed March 25, 2023. https://www.mkgandhi.org/articles/Gandhi%27s-Persuasive-Communication-and-Ideal-Journalism.html.

[2] Pletcher, Kenneth. "Salt March | Definition, Causes, History, & Facts." Encyclopedia Britannica, March 4, 2010. https://www.britannica.com/event/Salt-March.

[3] Boissoneault, Lorraine. "The Speech That Brought India to the Brink of Independence." Smithsonian Magazine, August 8, 2017. https://www.smithsonianmag.com/history/speech-brought-india-brink-independence-180964366/.

[4] Samur, Alexandra. "The History of Social Media in 33 Key Moments." Social Media Marketing & Management Dashboard, April 6, 2023. https://blog.hootsuite.com/history-social-media/.

32. Napoleon Bonaparte and AI Posture Correctors

[1] Godechot, Jacques. "Napoleon I | Biography, Achievements, & Facts." Encyclopedia Britannica, July 20, 1998. https://www.britannica.com/biography/Napoleon-I.

[2] Zelazko, Alicja. "Was Napoleon Short?" Encyclopedia Britannica, n.d. Accessed March 18, 2023. https://www.britannica.com/story/was-napoleon-short.

[3] Giordano, Medea. "7 Best Posture Correctors (2023): Braces, Apparel, Laptop Stands." WIRED, December 12, 2022. https://www.wired.com/gallery/posture-correctors/.

[4] Silver, Natalie. "How to Increase Your Height: Is There Any-

thing I Can Do?" Healthline, July 25, 2022. https://www.healthline.com/health/how-to-increase-height#how-to-increase-height.

33. Albert Einstein and Performance Socks

[1] WebMD. "What Are Signs of Genius?," May 25, 2021. https://www.webmd.com/balance/what-are-signs-of-genius.

[2] Encyclopedia Britannica. "Albert Einstein | Biography, Education, Discoveries, & Facts," April 14, 2023. https://www.britannica.com/biography/Albert-Einstein/Nazi-backlash-and-coming-to-America.

[3] ABC Radio National. "Why Einstein Didn't Wear Socks and the Nature of Scientific Inquiry." ABC Radio National, May 11, 2016. https://www.abc.net.au/radionational/programs/ockhamsrazor/einstein-socks-nature-scientific-inquiry/7395862.

[4] Reilly, Lucas. "19 Brilliant Facts About Albert Einstein." Mental Floss, March 14, 2023. https://www.mentalfloss.com/article/573985/albert-einstein-facts.

[5] Vermont, Darn Tough. "Making the Most Durable Socks." Darn Tough, December 6, 2022. https://darntough.com/blogs/the-alternate-stitch/making-most-durable-socks.

34. Frankenstein Novelist Mary Shelley and Dictation Software

[1] Wikipedia contributors. "Frankenstein." Wikipedia, September 2, 2001. https://en.wikipedia.org/wiki/Frankenstein.

[2] Kuiper, Kathleen. "Mary Wollstonecraft Shelley | Biography, Books, Frankenstein, Parents, & Facts." Encyclopedia Britannica, April 4, 2023. https://www.britannica.com/biography/Mary-Wollstonecraft-Shelley.

[3] Noblit, Clayton. "How to Dictate a Book in 2022 - Written Word Media." Written Word Media, March 14, 2022. https://www.writtenwordmedia.com/how-to-dictate-a-book/.

35. Gioachino Rossini and Truffle Burgers

[1] Caussou, Jean-Louis. "Gioachino Rossini | Italian Composer." Encyclopedia Britannica, July 20, 1998. https://www.britannica.com/biography/Gioachino-Rossini.

[2] Dodhia, Anjuli. "Good Music And Good Food: Cooking With Rossini." Northwest Public Broadcasting, March 8, 2018. https://www.nwpb.org/2018/03/09/good-music-good-food-cooking-rossini/.

[3] Huizenga, Tom. "Composers In The Kitchen: Gioachino Rossini's Haute Cuisine." NPR, November 25, 2010. https://www.npr.org/sections/deceptivecadence/2010/11/24/131568241/composers-in-the-kitchen-gioachino-rossini-s-haute-cuisine.

[4] Mathias, Shari. "10 Cool Rossini Facts." Parker Symphony Orchestra | Your Local Community Orchestra, January 31, 2022. https://parkersymphony.org/interesting-trivia-and-facts-about-rossini.

[5] Classic FM. "Gioachino Rossini: A Life," n.d. Accessed April 5, 2023. https://www.classicfm.com/composers/rossini/guides/discovering-great-composers-gioachino-rossini/.

[6] Walhout, Hannah. "A History of the Burger: From Ancient Rome to the Drive-Thru." Food & Wine, July 14, 2022. https://www.foodandwine.com/comfort-food/burgers/burger-timeline.

36. British Factory Workers and Digital Alarm Clocks

[1] The National Archives. "Victorian Industrial Towns - The National Archives," October 22, 2020. https://www.nationalarchives.gov.uk/education/resources/victorian-industrial-towns/.

[2] "Factories," n.d. Accessed March 27, 2023. https://www.bl.uk/learning/timeline/item106480.html.

[3] Peek, By Sitala. "Knocker Uppers: Waking up the Workers in Industrial Britain." BBC News, March 27, 2016. https://www.bbc.com/news/uk-england-35840393.

[4] Wikipedia contributors. "Knocker-Up." Wikipedia, April 14, 2023. https://en.wikipedia.org/wiki/Knocker-up.

[5] Burkhardt, Kai. "The Best Alarm Clocks of 2023." CNN Underscored, March 20, 2023. https://www.cnn.com/cnn-underscored/reviews/best-alarm-clocks.

37. Marilyn Monroe and Food Delivery Services

[1] Wong, Grant. "Who Was the Real Marilyn Monroe?" Smithsonian Magazine, September 26, 2022. https://www.smithsonianmag.com/history/who-was-the-real-marilyn-monroe-blonde-180980813/.

[2] Beschloss, Michael. "Marilyn Monroe's World War II Drone Program." The New York Times, June 3, 2014. https://www.nytimes.com/2014/06/04/upshot/marilyn-monroes-world-war-ii-drone-program.html.

[3] SanSone, Arricca Elin. "40 Rare Photos of Marilyn Monroe You've Probably Never Seen." Good Housekeeping, March 3, 2021. https://www.goodhousekeeping.com/life/entertainment/g28378198/rare-photos-of-marilyn-monroe/?slide=11.

[4] Conradt, Stacy. "30 Fascinating Facts About Marilyn Monroe." Mental Floss, September 30, 2022. https://www.mentalfloss.com/article/19268/14-breathless-facts-about-marilyn-monroe.

[5] Larkin, Isobel. "Marilyn Monroe's Rather Strange Diet Secrets Have Been Unearthed In An Old Interview." Women's Health, October 10, 2022. https://www.womenshealth.com.au/marilyn-monroe-diet/.

[6] Telegraph, Daily. "50 Things You Didn't Know About Marilyn." Business Insider, July 31, 2012. https://www.businessinsider.com/50-things-you-didnt-know-about-marilyn-2012-7.

[7] Lucas, Amelia. "Grubhub, Uber Eats and DoorDash Made Online Food Delivery a $10 Billion Business. Restaurants Aren't Happy about It." CNBC, December 16, 2019. https://www.cnbc.com/2019/12/13/grubhub-uber-eats-and-doordash-drove-an-online-food-delivery-boom.html.

38. Theodore Roosevelt and the Freezer

[1] The White House. "Theodore Roosevelt | The White House," December 23, 2022. https://www.whitehouse.gov/about-the-white-house/presidents/theodore-roosevelt/.

[2] Cooper, John Milton. "Theodore Roosevelt | Biography, Facts, Presidency, National Parks, & Accomplishments." Encyclopedia Britannica, April 3, 2023. https://www.britannica.com/biography/Theodore-Roosevelt.

[3] National Constitution Center – constitutioncenter.org. "10 Little-Known Facts about President Theodore Roosevelt," n.d. https://constitutioncenter.org/blog/10-little-known-facts-about-president-theodore-roosevelt.

[4] "The Hunter - Theodore Roosevelt Association," n.d. Accessed March 24, 2023. https://www.theodoreroosevelt.org/content.aspx?page_id=22&club_id=991271&module_id=339337.

[5] "PBS - Frontier House: Frontier Life," n.d. https://www.thirteen.org/wnet/frontierhouse/frontierlife/essay6_2.html.

[6] Olver, Lynne. "The Timeline--Presidents Food Favorites," n.d. Accessed March 24, 2023. https://www.foodtimeline.org/presidents.html#troosevelt.

[7] Organic, and Josh Dahlke. "The 7 Golden Rules of Wild Game Care, from Field to Freezer." Outdoor Life, April 20, 2021. https://www.outdoorlife.com/blogs/cast-iron-chef/7-golden-rules-wild-game-care-field-freezer/.

39. Sacagawea and the Pocket Translator

[1] Buckley, Jay H. "Lewis and Clark Expedition | Summary, History, Members, Facts, & Map." Encyclopedia Britannica, April 5, 2023. https://www.britannica.com/event/Lewis-and-Clark-Expedition.

[2] History.com. "Sacagawea: Facts, Tribe & Death - HISTORY," July 29, 2022. https://www.history.com/topics/native-american-history/sacagawea.

[3] Buckley, Jay H. "Sacagawea | Biography, Husband, Baby,

Death, & Facts." Encyclopedia Britannica, April 1, 2023. https://www.britannica.com/biography/Sacagawea.

40. King George VI and AI Voice Generator
[1] Stuttering Foundation: A Nonprofit Organization Helping Those Who Stutter. "King George," August 26, 2013. https://www.stutteringhelp.org/famous-people/king-george.
[2] British Pathé. "The Real King's Speech: King George VI's Stutter (1938) | British Pathé," July 28, 2011. https://www.youtube.com/watch?v=p1TubkzxPFY.
[3] The Editors of Encyclopaedia Britannica. "George VI | Stutter, Brother, & Death." Encyclopedia Britannica, March 27, 2023. https://www.britannica.com/biography/George-VI.
[4] Scott, Aileen. "A Guide To How Text-To-Speech Works." Data Science Central, August 22, 2022. https://www.datascience-central.com/a-guide-to-how-text-to-speech-works/.

41. Folk Musician Elizabeth Cotten and Music Streaming
[1] History.com. "U.S. Immigration Timeline: Definition & Reform - HISTORY," August 23, 2022. https://www.history.com/topics/immigration/immigration-united-states-timeline#irish-immigrant-wave.
[2] code:v_farquharson@kshira_interactive and j_nowicki@kshira_interactive design:k_wilson@framewerk. "PBS - American Roots Music : Eternal Songs - Folk Songs and Ballads," n.d. https://www.pbs.org/americanrootsmusic/pbs_arm_es_folkballad.html.
[3] MasterClass. "Folk Music Artists: A Brief History of Folk Music - 2023 - MasterClass," September 3, 2021. https://www.masterclass.com/articles/folk-music-guide.
[4] Smithsonian Folkways Recordings. "Elizabeth Cotten: Master of American Folk Music | Smithsonian Folkways Recordings," n.d. Accessed March 4, 2023. https://folkways.si.edu/elizabeth-cotten-master-american-folk/music/article/smithsonian.
[5] McCabe, Allyson. "How Elizabeth Cotten's Music Fu-

eled the Folk Revival." NPR, June 29, 2022. https://www.npr.
org/2022/06/29/1107090873/how-elizabeth-cottens-music-fu-
eled-the-folk-revival.

[6] Carley, Marika. "Libba Cotten's Guitar." Smithsonian Magazine, October 1, 2000. https://www.smithsonianmag.com/arts-cul-
ture/libba-cottens-guitar-32846747/.

[7] Wilson, Josh. "The Age Of Digital; Music Executive Re-
acts To The Impact Of Digitalization In The Music Industry."
Forbes, September 14, 2022. https://www.forbes.com/sites/
joshwilson/2022/09/14/the-age-of-digital-music-executive-re-
acts-to-the-impact-of-digitalization-in-the-music-indus-
try/?sh=243270d3537b.

[8] Take's Live Roots Music Channel. " TLRMC008 Elizabeth
Cotten 02/19/1975 Vol.2," December 15, 2015. https://www.you-
tube.com/watch?v=ujvSWRtEA6s.

42. Tao Porchon-Lynch and Smart Yoga Mats

[1] Albert, Victoria. "Tao Porchon-Lynch, Named World's Oldest Yoga Teacher, Has Died at 101." CBS News, February 22, 2020.
https://www.cbsnews.com/news/tao-porchon-lynch-worlds-old-
est-yoga-teacher-has-died-at-101/.

[2] Wikipedia contributors. "Tao Porchon-Lynch." Wikipedia,
March 2, 2023. https://en.wikipedia.org/wiki/Tao_Porchon-Lynch.

[3] Magazine, Westchester. "This 100-Year-Old Yoga Instructor Shares Her Extraordinary Life Story." Westchester Magazine,
February 25, 2020. https://westchestermagazine.com/life-style/
health/100-year-old-yoga-tao-porchon-lynch/.

[4] Yogapedia.com. "What Is Tao Porchon-Lynch? - Definition from Yogapedia," n.d. https://www.yogapedia.com/defini-
tion/5153/tao-porchon-lynch.

[5] Price, Emily. "This 'Smart' Yoga Mat Has a Built-In Instructor." Entrepreneur, November 6, 2014. https://www.entrepreneur.
com/science-technology/this-smart-yoga-mat-has-a-built-in-in-
structor/239398.

[6] Shivaraj. "YogiFi Landing - YogiFi." YogiFi, April 15, 2023. https://yogifi.fit/?v=7516fd43adaa.

43. Sigmund Freud and Smart Sofas

[1] Jay, Martin Evan. "Sigmund Freud | Biography, Theories, Psychology, Books, Works, & Facts." Encyclopedia Britannica, July 26, 1999. https://www.britannica.com/biography/Sigmund-Freud.

[2] Bradford, Alina. "Sigmund Freud: Life, Work & Theories." Livescience.Com, May 12, 2016. https://www.livescience.com/54723-sigmund-freud-biography.html.

[3] Biography. "Sigmund Freud," March 7, 2023. https://www.biography.com/scientists/sigmund-freud.

[4] Encyclopedia Britannica. "Sigmund Freud | Biography, Theories, Psychology, Books, Works, & Facts," July 26, 1999. https://www.britannica.com/biography/Sigmund-Freud/Psychoanalytic-theory.

[5] "Hypnosis, Medicine and Freud | Royal Society," n.d. Accessed February 26, 2023. https://royalsociety.org/blog/2017/05/hypnosis-medicine-and-freud/.

[6] WebMD Editorial Contributors. "What Is Psychoanalysis?" WebMD, April 15, 2021. https://www.webmd.com/mental-health/what-is-psychoanalysis.

44. Queen Victoria and Language Learning Apps

[1] Lingalot. "What Languages Did Queen Victoria Speak?," n.d. https://www.lingalot.com/what-languages-did-queen-victoria-speak/.

[2] Williams, Edgar Trevor, and Meredith Veldman. "Victoria | Biography, Family Tree, Children, Successor, & Facts." Encyclopedia Britannica, April 2, 2023. https://www.britannica.com/biography/Victoria-queen-of-United-Kingdom.

[3] Hunt, Kristin. "Victoria and Abdul: The Friendship That Scandalized England." Smithsonian Magazine, September 20, 2017. https://www.smithsonianmag.com/history/victoria-and-ab-

dul-friendship-scandalized-england-180964959/.

45. Buffalo Bill's Pony Express Rides and Email

[1] Boissoneault, Lorraine. "Murder, Marriage and the Pony Express: Ten Things You Didn't Know About Buffalo Bill." Smithsonian Magazine, January 10, 2017. https://www.smithsonianmag.com/history/murder-marriage-and-pony-express-10-things-you-didnt-know-about-buffalo-bill-180961736/.

[2] Encyclopedia Britannica. "Buffalo Bill | Biography & Facts," February 22, 2023. https://www.britannica.com/biography/William-F-Cody/The-Wild-West-show.

[3] Wikipedia contributors. "Pony Express." Wikipedia, April 11, 2023. https://en.wikipedia.org/wiki/Pony_Express.

[4] "The Story Of The Pony Express | National Postal Museum," n.d. Accessed March 21, 2023. https://postalmuseum.si.edu/research/articles-from-enroute/the-story-of-the-pony-express.html.

[5] Encyclopedia Britannica. "Pony Express - The First Delivery," July 20, 1998. https://www.britannica.com/topic/Pony-Express/The-first-delivery.

46. Politicians and AI Political Speech Writing Technology

[1] Wikipedia contributors. "Orator (Cicero)." Wikipedia, January 22, 2021. https://en.wikipedia.org/wiki/Orator_(Cicero).

[2] Wikipedia contributors. "Catilinarian Orations." Wikipedia, March 25, 2023. https://en.wikipedia.org/wiki/Catilinarian_orations.

[3] Yonge, Charles Duke, trans. "Cicero: First Speech against Catiline." Accessed April 8, 2023. https://www.sjsu.edu/people/cynthia.rostankowski/courses/HUM1AF14/s3/Lecture-26-Cicero-and-Caesar-Reading.pdf.

[4] CBC. "Political Speeches Aren't Boring by Accident, Says Graham Steele," April 7, 2016. https://www.cbc.ca/news/canada/nova-scotia/graham-steele-column-apr7-1.3525543.

[5] O'Dea, Michaela. "How To Write A Political Speech," n.d. Accessed April 8, 2023. https://www.ecanvasser.com/blog/political-speeches.

[6] arXiv, Emerging Technology From The. "How an AI Algorithm Learned to Write Political Speeches." MIT Technology Review, April 2, 2020. https://www.technologyreview.com/2016/01/19/163831/how-an-ai-algorithm-learned-to-write-political-speeches/.

[7] CALVIN WOODWARD and JOSH BOAK Associated Press and ABC News. "ChatGPT Bot Channels History to Pen State of Union Speech." ABC News, February 6, 2023. https://abcnews.go.com/Business/wireStory/chatgpt-bot-channels-history-pen-state-union-speech-96916882.